The Return of Heaven

Steve Martin

Cover design and layout by Choregeo Media

www.TheReturnofHeaven.com

ISBN 979-8-9946248-1-4

Printed in the United States of America

Choregeo Media

Tyler, Texas

ACKNOWLEDGMENTS

The idea for this book started germinating in my mind back when I was 14 years old. Through the years there have been many people who have impacted my life in such a way that has left their fingerprints somewhere on the pages of this book.

So, thank you to my family.
To:

Angela — my lovely wife and faithful partner

Mom & Dad — who showed the way (Mom, I miss you)

My children — Heaven's mirror. Your lives show me what I really look like.

My wonderful siblings and their spouses. (Donna, we miss you)

My gratitude also extends to the reviewers, editors, and early readers who helped refine these ideas and bring clarity to the message. Your insight, questions, and faith sharpened every chapter... more than you know.

Thanks to the men in my life who came alongside me and left your mark both on me and in me. God bless you.

In Memory of:

Johnny Miller — you cast the vision for who I could be.

Dick Frey — you walked with me through hard times. You modeled how to give grace.

Dale West — humble yet mighty. Your faith moved mountains.

Al McCallister — you made learning cool.

Finally, to every reader who longs for something more — for a world made right and a life made new — may this book draw your heart toward the One who makes all things new. If we don't meet in this life, come find me when we get to the other side.

DEDICATION

Dedicated to my grandchildren.

I wrote this book to you, and for you.

Estie
Rhodes
Callum
Isobel
Avalee
Lincoln
Shephard
Isaiah

In Memory of
Jameson

You changed us all. We love you buddy!

"When you come looking for me, you'll find me.
Yes — when you get serious about finding me and want it more than anything else,
I'll make sure you won't be disappointed."

— Jeremiah 29:13 (MSG)

Contents

Chapter 1

What in the World Is Going On?

A few years ago, my then four-year-old granddaughter was on a camping trip with her aunts, uncles, and cousins. It was one of those rare days when everything just seemed right. The river was wide and lazy. The kids swam, raced kayaks, played water games, and roasted hot dogs around a fire. There were s'mores, belly laughs, and more love in the air than bugs (which is saying something for a Texas summer). It was the kind of day that makes you believe, even just for a moment, that all is well.

But then came the night.

Everyone bedded down in tents scattered around the campsite. The stars were out. The fire had died down. And then the sounds began—frogs and crickets, buzzing cicadas, coyotes howling somewhere off in the distance, the steady noise of the river rolling by, even a nearby roost of wild turkeys flapping and chattering like a tree full of squabbling cousins.

In the middle of all that beautiful chaos, my granddaughter sat upright on her cot, looked around, and said (in that perfect little-kid voice that carries through canvas walls):

"What in the world is going on?"

There was a pause, then a tent-wide eruption of adult laughter. It was the perfect question. That little girl had stumbled into a mystery most of us never grow out of. A world that had felt safe and joyful just hours before now felt...strange. Loud. Unknown.

If we're honest, that same question lives inside every one of us.

What in the world is going on?

We ask it when a relationship shatters.

We whisper it at funerals.

We scream it in hospital rooms.

We cry it in courtrooms.

We sigh it quietly after another night of bad news.

We live in a world that doesn't quite add up. Some moments feel like heaven—a perfect day on the river, a wedding, the first time you hold your child. But those moments never last. The world always breaks back through.

I still remember being a preschooler, waiting for Christmas morning with heart-pounding excitement. For weeks, I had dreamed about what was under the tree—and that year, I got everything I wanted. There were even a few surprises. For a moment, everything felt like magic. But then, almost as soon as the presents were unwrapped—I remember sitting there, feeling . . . off, like something wasn't quite right. I couldn't explain it, but it was there—a quiet emptiness. As if, even at five years old, I was already asking, "Is this it?"

That feeling grows up with us.

The stories get harder.

The wonder fades.

And the ache deepens.

Families split. Marriages betray. Promises break. The very people who were supposed to protect us sometimes become the ones who wound us most. People use us. Abandon us. We lose jobs. We lose trust. We lose the people we love. And through it all, something inside us keeps crying out:

This is not the way it's supposed to be.

And you know what? That voice is right.

We were made for more than this. We were designed for something good—something whole, lasting, and real. But somewhere along the way, it broke. And now, like children waking up in a noisy campground after the fire's gone out, we find ourselves blinking into the darkness, wondering what happened to the world we thought we knew.

We want heaven.

We just want it on our own terms.

That's the catch. Deep down, we know there's something more. Call it heaven. Call it peace. Call it home. Whatever name you give it, our hearts are wired for it. Yet instead of trusting the One who made us for it, we try to build it ourselves—out of careers, romance, success, comfort, power, religion, politics, or anything else we believe might fill the gap.

But those things can't hold the weight we place on them. So we end up living in a world full of people chasing the eternal with tools that were never meant to last.

It's no wonder things feel upside down.

No wonder we ache.

No wonder we keep asking, "What in the world is going on?"

In this book, we'll look at the bigger story—a story that began before time and stretches into eternity. It's a story of heaven, lost and restored. A story that makes sense of the longing in your heart and the pain in your world. It starts with something good, it breaks, and then—somehow—it's made right again.

You're not crazy to feel like something is off.

You're not wrong to hope there's more.

There is.

And it's more real than you could ever imagine.

Chapter 2

Ground Rules

I f you're going to take a long journey, you need more than a destination. You need a map and a compass that points north.

This chapter is that compass.

If you're going to play a game, you need a shared set of rules. These are ours.

If you're going to have a conversation, words must carry shared meaning. You may not agree with every definition, but if we're to communicate, we need to speak the same language.

I'm not here to win an argument or flex credentials. You won't find endless footnotes, charts, or dense philosophy.

What you will find is a story—the biggest one there is. It's the true story of reality, revealed by the God who made us.

You are free to question it, wrestle with it, or even walk away. But if you're willing to keep walking with me, this chapter will show you the foundation I'm building on—the lens through which I view everything that follows.

This is the foundation I'm standing on—the story I believe is true.

God

We could spend a lifetime exploring this, but here are a few key truths that form the foundation of everything else in this story.

God is love. That is not a soft phrase or poetic ideal—it is the starting point of all reality. Real love cannot be forced. It allows freedom, and freedom requires choice. True choices carry real consequences, and that one truth explains much of what has gone wrong in the world.

God is just. If love introduces the reality of choice, and choice leads to consequences, then justice is necessary. God's justice ensures that those consequences fit the choices made. Love and justice are not opposites; they are two parts of the same whole.

God is wise. This world does not spin without purpose. God has a plan. He sees the beginning and the end all at once. His wisdom is limitless, and He brings His purposes to completion in their proper time. Our lives are only a few paragraphs in one chapter of a vast story. Trying to judge the scope of His wisdom from our limited viewpoint is like trying to understand a novel by reading only a single sentence.

God exists as Trinity. God is one Being in three Persons—not a team, not a disguise, not a math error.

Picture three candles pushed so close their flames merge into one. Still three wicks. One fire. Same light.

Each Person in this Trinity plays a role:

- First Person—the architect.

- Second Person—the builder (every time God steps into the world, it's Him).

- Third Person—the quiet force (conviction, comfort, chaos-control).

It's bigger than we can grasp. It may stretch the mind but it's no illusion.

God is deeply personal. He formed you in the womb, knows every detail about you, and desires that you know Him in return. He invites you to walk with Him, to love Him, and to be known by Him. This relationship lies at the heart of The Return of Heaven.

Revelation

God has not left us in the dark.

He reveals Himself in two primary ways:

General revelation.

This is what you see in nature, in beauty, and in the quiet pull of conscience. It's the awe you feel beneath a canopy of stars or the wonder that fills you when you hold a newborn. It's that inner voice insisting, "This isn't right," or the whisper reminding you, "All of this didn't just happen."

General revelation cannot stand alone. Its truths point us toward God—and lead us into His special revelation.

Special Revelation.

This is God speaking more clearly and directly—*through Scripture.* That is where this story finds its backbone.

One thing to keep in mind as you read: this book is not special revelation, but it can point you toward it. God has promised, "If you seek me with all your heart, you will find me."[1]

The truth is before us—we only need to look for it.

It may begin small: in the beauty of a sunset, in the realization that design implies a Designer, or in the moral law that echoes across every culture and age.

As we acknowledge these glimpses, He draws us closer. And in time, we find ourselves face-to-face with what Scripture reveals.

As one writer put it, He takes us "further in."
(C.S. Lewis, The Last Battle)

When we seek Him with all our heart, we find Him.

But if we choose to close our eyes to what He has revealed—if we ignore the evidence of His hand in creation, the whisper of conscience, or the truth found in Scripture—God allows us that freedom. In time, He gives us what we insist on: our own way.

We may reject revelation or we may pursue it.

But we cannot say it was never given.

Heaven

Since this book centers on heaven, let's define what we mean from the start. Heaven is not simply clouds, harps, or a vague spiritual afterlife.

Heaven is God's space—the realm where His will is done completely. It is real, relational, and more solid than we imagine. It exists both now and in the future.

Heaven is not only the place faithful followers go when they die. It is what humanity lost, what we still long for, and what will one day be restored.

Scripture uses the word heaven in several distinct ways:

The sky above, where the birds fly

The cosmos beyond, where the stars dwell

The unseen spiritual realm, where invisible beings operate

God's present dwelling place, where His throne resides

The Eternal City—the future union of heaven and earth, a restored creation where God, His spiritual hosts, and humanity live together in harmony

It's natural to ask—if the Eternal City is still in the future, what happens to those who have already died?

The short answer: death's address has changed over time.

Early on, everyone went to Sheol—a shadowy waiting room with two sides: comfort and torment.

Then, at a turning point (we'll unpack this later), the comfort side was emptied into God's presence—now called Paradise. The torment side stayed—now Hades.

But the Eternal City is the destination. That's the Return of Heaven we're chasing.

The Spiritual Realm

There is more to reality than what we can see or measure.

The Bible describes a world alive with spiritual beings—some loyal to God, others in rebellion. They are not myths or metaphors but real entities whose story intersects deeply with our own.

These beings carry different roles, ranks, and titles. "Angel" is only one of those roles, yet over time, we have come to use it as a catch-all term.

Angels are not a race. They do not marry, reproduce, or have children. Each is a distinct creation of God.

By contrast, God created Adam and Eve as the beginning of the human race, and from them came all humanity. That distinction matters, because it shapes our place in the larger story. We'll see how their world and ours connect as the story unfolds.

Mankind

Humanity was made in the image of God—endowed with dignity, creativity, and eternal purpose.

We are not eternal—we had a beginning. But we are everlasting—we will have no end. And that sets us apart from the rest of creation.

Yet something within us has broken. We have become disconnected from the source of life. We are not what we were meant to be, and we know it. Every ache for meaning, every longing for home, echoes that truth.

As Scripture reminds us, humanity is one race—one family sharing a common nature and story. That shared story matters deeply, because it determines where we have come from and where we are going.

One Last Word

For some, reading this chapter may have been a review, but for many it probably felt like drinking from a firehose. We've been talking about an all-wise, infinite Creator. How could it not feel overwhelming?

But remember: God is deeply personal. He wants you to know Him. And He promises that if we seek Him with all our heart, we will find Him.[1]

Even if we spent a lifetime learning about the ways of God, we'd barely scratch the surface. He's infinite. Yet He meets us where we are. Exactly where we are. If we're seeking, since He knows who we are and what we need, He reveals Himself in ways that meet us in each moment.

Walking with God is like ascending a spiral staircase. Some days it feels like we're right back where we started—coming full circle, wondering if we've made any progress. But whether we realize it or not, each time we circle around, we're a little higher than before.

As I tell the story of God's plan, I'll be living in the tension of giving you enough to follow and connect the dots without overwhelming you with the endless depth of His wisdom and ways. At times, you might feel like it's too much; other times, not enough.

And that's okay. This story is meant to be entered, not conquered in a single reading. For those moments when your questions feel heavier than the page can carry, just know this: there is a place beyond this book where the conversation can continue. When the time is right, I'll show you where to find it.

We all struggle in this life—some more than others. And too often, the people we'd normally turn to are the same ones who've added to our pain or confusion.

But that ache you feel—the sense that something's off—isn't without meaning.

Maybe you have always sensed that something is off, that the world is not as it should be. Perhaps you have wondered why, even in moments of joy, there remains an ache for something more.

This book is here to help you understand that feeling. You are not alone, and you are not imagining it.

Because the world is filled with pain, fear, and loss, many of us grow angry with God. That anger is understandable. When suffering presses close, words often fail. But if you have carried that anger and still chosen to open this book, there is hope. Be open to His revelation, and He will show you more.

Remember that love requires choice, and choices bring consequences. Those consequences shape the world around us. God sees them all, and through His love, His choices, and His wisdom, He will make everything right again.

Faith is the firm foundation beneath all that gives life meaning. It is the unseen anchor that allows us to trust what we cannot yet see. Anyone who comes to God must believe that He exists and that He responds to those who truly seek Him.[2]

A moment from Avengers: Endgame comes to mind. When all seems lost—Iron Man fallen, Thor defeated, and Captain America standing alone—he hears that quiet voice in his ear: "On your left." Hope returns. So hold on.

Now, let's return to the story.

Chapter 3

What Is Truth?

I f we're going to talk about matters of heaven and eternity, we need to look at them through an eternal lens of truth.

In today's culture, many people have embraced the idea that truth is personal—that each of us can have our own version of it. But that belief begins to crumble the moment we examine it closely. So let's take a look at a few of the ways this idea tends to show up.

If it doesn't feel true to me, then it can't be true at all.

That's where many of us live these days, even if we don't admit it. Truth has become something personal and customizable, shaped by our experiences and emotions. Like your coffee order or your favorite playlist, it's all about what works for you.

But here's the problem: not everything that feels true is true, and not everything that is true feels good.

Truth and a Screaming Toddler

Have you ever taken a small child to the doctor for a routine visit, knowing there will be that dreaded moment of "the stick"? Perhaps a blood draw? Or maybe you remember being that child yourself.

You know exactly how it goes. The nurse walks in with a tray. The child senses something is wrong. The needle appears—and then comes the meltdown.

The child screams, cries, and looks at you as if you've betrayed them forever. From their perspective, you're the bad guy. How could you let this happen?

But from your perspective, you're protecting them. You're allowing the blood draw to help confirm potential issues with their body—maybe even save their life one day. You know things they don't. You see a bigger picture.

The truth is, that moment of pain is good for them. But the experience hurts, and because it hurts, they can't believe it's good.

We often react to God in the same way.

We hit painful moments in life and assume something has gone wrong—that God must have dropped the ball, or worse, that He doesn't care. But what if He sees the bigger picture? What if we're responding with the limited understanding of a frightened child, while God is the good parent holding our hand?

In my experience, this has often been the root of many who profess atheism. Some grew up in homes where disbelief was simply inherited. But many others turned away from God because of deep emotional pain. Almost as if to punish Him, they say in their hearts, "You weren't there for me. You let this happen. Fine, then—you're gone from my life."

Yet when they push down that pain, trying to ignore or bury it, they also bury their awareness of God. The truth is, He remains—quietly present in the very place they refuse to look—waiting for the moment they are willing to face their pain and find Him again.

If we define truth only by what we can see or feel in the moment, we will miss the deeper work God is doing. We will stunt our growth and lose sight of the larger story He is writing.

Truth is always bigger than our feelings about it.

Truth Is Relative

This is another idea that's become popular today—the belief that everyone gets to define their own truth. You've probably heard people say things like, "This is my truth," "Your truth is valid," or "Live your truth."

It sounds kind. It feels tolerant. But when we follow that idea to its logical conclusion, it begins to collapse under its own weight.

I once heard Ravi Zacharias share a story that still makes me smile.

He's from India, but two American professors were schooling him on "Eastern logic": "Truth can be both/and, not just either/or."

Ravi just said, "Friends, when an Indian crosses the road, he looks both ways. Because it's *either* him *or* the truck. Not both/and."

Point made—with a grin.

We can debate which ice cream flavor is best, but that's a matter of opinion, not truth.

If we're standing in the middle of the road debating whether a truck is coming, that's no longer an opinion. The truck is *either* coming *or* it's not.

Francis Schaeffer saw this in the '60s in *The God Who Is There*.[1] He said we built a two-story house for truth:

- Downstairs: facts, science, what you can measure.

- Upstairs: meaning, faith, "your truth."

Problem? If God's real, He's not upstairs. He's the whole house—gravity, stars, *you*. We all feel the pull. He's not a flavor. He's the truck.

If someone stands in traffic and sincerely believes there is no truck coming, it is not kindness to say, "Well, that's their truth." If the truck is coming, it's coming—and denying it will not stop it.

And what happens when "your truth" contradicts "my truth"? What if "my truth" harms someone else? What if neither of us actually knows what's real?

Suddenly, the idea of personal truth doesn't feel so safe or enlightened. It feels fragile, uncertain—built on shifting sand.

If we're going to talk about heaven, or anything eternal, we need something more solid than that. Real truth—what Francis Schaeffer called True-truth—is the kind that stands firm under pressure. It has to be true for everyone, not just true for me.

The Stereogram Analogy

You've probably seen one of those stereogram pictures—images that look like random chaos at first, a blur of dots and swirls. Yet hidden inside is a three-dimensional image.

When we view the world's brokenness through a relative idea of truth, all we see is confusion. We invent a worldview to help us cope, even if it's guesswork.

But truth isn't like modern art, open to interpretation. It's like the stereogram. There really is an image there. At first, it's frustrating. Your eyes resist. But once you learn to look beyond the surface, the picture comes into focus. It's not imagination. It's real—and the same for everyone.(Not familiar with a stereogram? Go to thereturnofheaven.com/truth. There is one posted there for you to check out)

That's what truth is like. Not something we create, but something we uncover. Not a feeling or a vote, but a reality waiting to be revealed.

Those who still see only chaos may be offended when someone insists there's a picture. But those who've seen it know it's there for all. Their insistence isn't arrogance—it's compassion, a warning that the truck really is coming.

Truth doesn't change because it's ignored or unpopular. When we begin to see life through God's eternal perspective, His truth comes into focus—solid, real, and unshakable.

Truth Doesn't Always Reveal Itself on Our Timeline

There's one more thing to say about truth: sometimes it takes time to see.

If you've ever jumped into a story halfway through, you know how confusing it can be. Think about watching a long, connected series like *Stranger Things* or *The Mandalorian*. If you start in the middle, it can look like everything's falling apart—heroes scattered, worlds collapsing, and darkness closing in. You'd probably wonder what kind of story this is and why it seems to be ending so badly.

But someone who knows the bigger arc—who's seen what came before and knows what's coming after—understands that this isn't the end. It's a turning point. A necessary step in the greater redemption that's already been written.

Truth sometimes works the same way.

We hit a painful moment and assume, That's it. That's the whole story. But we're stepping into the middle of a chapter and trying to evaluate the entire book. We can't see the full timeline. We don't know how this moment fits into God's larger plan.

But God does.

If truth is based only on what we can grasp right now, we'll always be misled. But if we trust that God sees what we don't—that He knows the whole timeline—we can live in the tension with hope.

Only when we see truth through God's eternal perspective will we be ready to understand—and to long for—the return of Heaven.

Note: Ravi Zacharias' later personal failures were serious and heartbreaking. They don't erase the truth of the illustrations he shared, but they are a reminder that even those who defend truth can fall short of living it. In fact, Ravi's life—like all of ours—underscores the very point of Chapter 1, What in the World Is Going On?, and helps draw attention to the need for the story that follows in this book.

Chapter 4

The World That Was

The State of God's Creation

In the beginning, God spoke time, space, and matter into existence—the physical universe. Before this moment, He had already created the unseen spiritual realm and the beings who dwell within it. Then God shaped the earth, filling it with life in all its beauty and variety. At the pinnacle of His creation, He formed something unique: human beings, His image-bearers.

Adam and Eve were not gods, yet they reflected God's nature in a way nothing else could. They were self-aware, moral beings with the ability to reason, choose, and love. They could mirror His moral goodness, His creativity, His joy in beauty, and His capacity for selfless love.

The world they entered was perfect, yet untamed. It was not a manicured garden but a living, breathing masterpiece waiting for its care. Rivers laughed over rocks. Forests whispered in the wind. The very air seemed alive with promise.

At the heart of this new world, God planted a special garden—Eden—the place where heaven and earth touched. There, God Himself walked among His image-bearers, face to face.

Life in Eden was designed to last forever. There was no genetic corruption, no disease, no decay. The environment was tuned for abundance. It may have been sheltered by a water canopy high in the atmosphere, creating a gentle, uniform climate. This canopy could have filtered harmful rays from the sun and enriched the air with oxygen so pure that every breath felt like new life. Imagine tasting fruit that had never known rot, drinking water so clear it seemed like liquid light, and hearing the rustle of trees that had never felt the touch of death.

Our Struggle to Imagine It

We can hardly picture such a world. Even our best dreams are smudged by the reality we know. Scripture describes our view of what will one day be as looking into a dim mirror—the image is there, but blurred.[1] It's also compared to staring at a seed you have never seen before and trying to imagine the tree it will become.[2]

It's like someone who has been colorblind from birth. They think they see the whole world until someone hands them special glasses. You've likely seen those videos online—people putting them on for the first time. Suddenly, colors burst into view, shades they never even knew existed. Many react with tears, laughter, or stunned silence as they realize the world has always been richer, deeper, and more beautiful than they could have imagined. That's what it would be like to see Eden again.

That is the challenge of this chapter. It's like a colorblind person trying to describe color to someone who is also colorblind. There is no frame of reference. They don't know what color is. In the same way, describing a world without corruption, decay, or death—and relationships of pure love without fear, agendas, or manipulation—is almost impossible because we have nothing to compare it to.

Yet God has given us glimpses, even if we cannot fully understand them. The "world that was" did not last long, but He has revealed enough for us to catch flashes of it—echoes from the beginning of time and hints of the heaven and earth yet to come.

A Wild but Perfect World

Adam and Eve were given authority to rule over the earth. They were not merely gardeners; they were king and queen of the physical realm, entrusted with all of God's creation. The world was flawless—no death, no decay, no disease—but it was not finished. It was wild in the best possible way, bursting with life and possibility, waiting for their touch to bring harmony, beauty, and design.

Their mission was fourfold: to rule, subdue, cultivate, and keep.

To rule: meant exercising authority to guide creation and shape the path of civilization.

To subdue: not to crush creation but to bring its wildness into order, revealing greater beauty.

To cultivate: meant drawing out its hidden potential, nurturing life into fullness.

To keep: to guard and protect it from harm.

Work in Eden was not about survival. There was no struggle against scarcity, no exhaustion from labor. Every effort was creative, joyful, and filled with purpose. Their energy was spent entirely on exploration, discovery, and invention. Every task brought delight; every day was an adventure.

Even in our broken world, think of what men and women have achieved even under the weight of decay: cities carved from stone, cathedrals reaching toward the heavens, music that stirs the soul, medicine that saves lives, and technology that connects continents. Consider the rebuilding of nations after war or the compassion shown when disaster strikes. Picture the pyramids of Egypt, the Great Wall of China, Michelangelo's Sistine Chapel, Beethoven's symphonies, or the breathtaking images sent back from the Hubble telescope.

And then think of the feats of courage and love—firefighters running into burning towers, nations sending aid after earthquakes, families opening their homes to children not their own.

Even the Apollo moon landing, an impossible dream realized in less than a decade through a shared vision, is but one glimpse.

Now multiply all of that by a thousand, and you begin to approach what Eden could have been: a civilization where every person was healthy, whole, and united in a common mission of beauty and discovery, working in a world that did not resist them but flourished with them.

Perfect Relationship, Perfect Freedom

Adam and Eve's physical, emotional, intellectual, and spiritual life flowed directly from God, like branches drawing life from a vine. Because He was their source of love, security, and meaning, they were free to love without fear and to give without needing to protect themselves. Their worth was not something they earned or proved; it simply existed because they were connected to Him.

From that perfect union with God flowed a perfect relationship with each other. There was no insecurity, no suspicion, no manipulation—only complete openness and trust.

Think of the first days of falling in love, when every word and every glance deepens connection and delight. In Eden, that was not a fleeting experience but the continual rhythm of life together.

When Adam and Eve became one, they became more than the sum of their parts. Two lives joined to create something exponentially greater. Physically, their union could bring forth new life, but it also produced new life in other ways—emotionally, intellectually, and spiritually. Together, they generated fresh ideas, relationships, and dreams. They did not have to compromise to agree; they harmonized. From that harmony came creation itself—beauty, wisdom, and progress born from unity.

Imagine every human relationship working that way—each one perfectly aligned—building, solving, exploring, and designing together. In such a world, nothing would be impossible. Every form of connection, from marriage to community, would be marked by that same supernatural synergy.

Relationship with the Creatures

In Eden, death did not exist—not even among the animals. Every creature fed on plants, and fear was unknown. Imagine walking among a herd of wild animals without danger, or feeling the warmth of a lion's breath as it lay beside a lamb. The animals were not domesticated, yet they were not wild in the way we know wildness. The entire creation moved in harmony, each life at peace with every other.

The Garden at the Center

Beyond Eden, the world was still young. Rivers were tracing their paths through untouched soil, trees were stretching toward heaven, and life was multiplying across the earth. Into this new and vibrant world, God planted a garden—the dwelling place of His image-bearers and the meeting point of heaven and earth.

Here, God walked with them and spoke with them. His presence was not a mystery or a hope; it was a daily reality. The divide between the physical and spiritual worlds did not yet exist. Encounters with spiritual beings were as natural as breathing, as familiar as the morning light.

Modern science paints a picture of humanity climbing upward, evolving into higher forms. Scripture tells the opposite story. We began at the height of strength and wisdom, the pinnacle of creation, and have declined ever since. Adam and Eve were likely stronger, more intelligent, and more imaginative than any of us—unhindered by decay, fear, or confusion.

They lived in a perfect world, surrounded by perfect relationships, flourishing in discovery and creativity, and walking each day with their Creator.

This was the world that was—the heaven on earth humanity was meant to rule. But as the next chapter reveals, something went terribly wrong, and the story of the world changed forever.

Chapter 5

Rebellion

Setting the Stage

Before we can understand rebellion, we need to see the stage on which it unfolded. When most people hear the word angel, they picture glowing figures with wings. Yet in Scripture, "angel" is only one role among a vast and varied company of unseen beings. The word itself simply means messenger.

Some of these beings are called cherubim—guardians placed at sacred thresholds to protect what matters most. Others are seraphim—worshipers whose voices shake the heavens as they proclaim God's glory. Scripture also speaks of the sons of God—created beings, members of a divine council who serve and advise under His authority. Then there are the angels themselves—messengers sent on divine missions, sometimes to deliver God's word, other times to carry out His judgment. Among them are archangels, warrior-leaders who stand at the front lines when conflict erupts in the unseen realm.

God crafted each of these beings with intention and individuality. They were not identical creations stamped in uniformity but unique beings reflecting the Creator's imagination. Just as humanity was entrusted with stewardship of the visible world, these celestial beings were given authority within the invisible one. And like humanity, they too possessed the ability to choose.

From this vast company, one figure stood apart. He was radiant, powerful, and honored above many. His name was Lucifer—a guardian of surpassing beauty and privilege. His role was one of honor and authority, but pride twisted into ambition. He longed not just to reflect God's glory but to rival it. Within him, the first seeds of rebellion began to take root.

The First Rebellion

That ambition led to the first great fracture in creation and a number of the members of the spiritual realm joined Lucifer in open defiance.

Lucifer's rebellion did not begin with thunder or fire. His first loss was not his place in heaven, but something quieter—and in many ways, far more tragic. He lost his purpose. Once the "anointed cherub who covers," radiant with splendor and entrusted with glory, he turned from his calling and became consumed by pride. What had been beauty became corruption. What had been protection became accusation.

Even after his fall, Scripture shows that Lucifer still had access to the courts of heaven. In Scripture—in the book of Job, he appears before God to accuse the righteous.[1] In the writings of Zechariah, he again points his finger at God's people.[2] He was no longer the guardian but the accuser—still present, yet fallen in purpose.

As he took on this new identity, what Scripture called him changed. In Hebrew, the word Satan means "adversary" or "accuser." Over time, his role became his name: Satan.

Later, at a decisive turning point in human history—one we will soon explore—everything shifted. Scripture describes this moment as Satan being "cast down," stripped of his role as accuser, and no longer permitted to stand before God's throne.[3] Though he still prowls as an adversary, his standing in the heavens was permanently changed. His fall unfolded in stages: first in position, then in authority, and finally in access.

Yet the rebellion was not complete until it reached earth—until humanity's choice became part of the story.

Love and Choice

Here we return to a theme woven through all of creation: love and freedom. God created humanity with the ability to choose—granting the power to love and be loved. Because God is love, He desires that His creation experience a genuine relationship with Him and with one another. But true love cannot exist without choice.

And real choice carries real consequences. A just and perfect God ensures that consequences always fit the choice—if not in this life, then in the time when every hidden thing is brought to light. Humanity now stood before a defining decision, one that would test their trust in God's character.

The Temptation

This moment opens on a curious scene. Eve walks through the garden, and a legged serpent approaches her. She doesn't seem alarmed that it speaks. Instead, they converse naturally.

It's important to remember that this takes place in "the world that was"—a realm where heaven and earth met. In Eden, Adam and Eve likely encountered spiritual and physical beings we no longer see today. The moment feels almost like something from C. S. Lewis's Chronicles of Narnia—a world alive with mystery and meaning.

Scripture calls the serpent "more cunning than any other creature."[4] Later, we learn that this was Lucifer himself. Was he disguised, or did he inhabit one of God's creatures? We cannot know for certain, but the narrative suggests the latter, since God later addresses both Lucifer and the serpent in His judgment.

What we do know is that Lucifer began spinning a subtle lie—questioning God's word, twisting His truth, and suggesting that perhaps God was withholding something good.

In the garden stood many trees, but two were unique: the Tree of Life and the Tree of the Knowledge of Good and Evil. God's command was clear: they could eat from any tree except the latter. "The day you eat of it, you will surely die,"[5] He warned.

Lucifer contradicted God. He told Eve that she would not die, that instead her eyes would be opened and she would become like God. Doubt took root. She began to question God's intentions, His love, and His truthfulness.

In that moment, Eve faced a choice—to love and trust God, or to follow her own understanding and Lucifer's deception. Eve chose not to trust the good God who'd only ever been good to her. Instead, she chose to trust in herself, and in the cunning serpent she'd only just met. Then she gave the fruit to Adam, who was with her. Eve was deceived, but Adam's sin was deliberate.

Scripture makes this clear: "She took of its fruit and ate, and she also gave some to her husband who was with her".[6] Adam wasn't distant or unaware. He stood beside her, seeing the choice and its cost, yet he remained silent and joined her in disobedience.

And in that instant, everything changed.

Adam and Eve's Choice

Lucifer's deception succeeded—but not in the same way for both. Eve was deceived. Adam was not.

This distinction matters. Eve was misled; Adam abdicated. He surrendered the authority and responsibility God had entrusted to him.

Scripture is precise in its wording: "She took of its fruit and ate, and she also gave some to her husband who was with her, and he ate".[6] Adam was there. He was not tricked or absent. He watched, understood the weight of the choice, and still joined her in rebellion.

In that moment, everything shifted. Harmony gave way to fracture. Freedom became bondage. Life surrendered to death.

The break ran deeper than the soil beneath their feet; it reached into the very fabric of their relationship.

Eve, now painfully aware of her vulnerability, struggled between trust and control. To trust Adam meant becoming even more vulnerable. To seize control meant living in isolation. Either choice fractured the harmony that once defined their bond.

Adam, burdened by shame and failure, withdrew into his labor. Yet work was no longer joy or discovery—it became toil and survival. The same ground that once yielded abundance now resisted him with thorns and futility.

What had been a relationship of selfless love and mutual devotion became one of negotiation and guardedness. Each sought to fill an emptiness the other could not reach, trying to draw from one another what only their Creator could supply.

The union that once made them greater together than apart dissolved into two individuals, self-protective and estranged, each reaching for control. And though we may protest that our relationships are not like this, we must remember that we see only in part. Like those born colorblind, we perceive the grayscale version of what for Adam and Eve was full color. We cannot comprehend the depth of intimacy and trust they once shared.

The Consequences

The Serpent

God's first words of judgment were not directed at Adam or Eve, but at the serpent. At first glance, the words seem to condemn an animal, yet beneath that surface lies a far deeper meaning. The serpent was not the true enemy—it was the vessel of one.

The curse came in layers. The creature itself would crawl in the dust, a visible symbol of humiliation and deceit. But the judgment reached beyond its scales and movement. God was addressing the power behind it—Lucifer, now fallen and exposed as Satan.

From that moment, a divine decree was set in motion. Enmity would exist between the serpent and the woman, and between her descendants. This was not a single act of vengeance but the beginning of a conflict that would stretch across all generations—a war between deception and truth, darkness and light.

The Woman

Eve's part in the rebellion carried its own weight of consequence. The judgment fell upon the very heart of her design: to bring forth life and to live in harmony with her husband. What would have been pure joy in childbirth would now be intertwined with pain. What was once a perfect partnership would now hold tension, the struggle between love and control woven into the fabric of human relationships.

The Man and the Ground

Adam's disobedience brought not only personal loss but cosmic consequence. The ground he was called to cultivate now resisted him. Labor became toil. The joy of creation turned to exhaustion. What once yielded abundance now gave back thorns and dust.

And death, once foreign to creation, entered as a grim inheritance. The man formed from the soil would one day return to it. The harmony of life had been broken, and the shadow of mortality began its long dominion.

The Fallout

In that moment, death entered the story—not suddenly, but in layers. Humanity is more than flesh and bone. We are bodies, formed from the dust. We are souls, made of thought, emotion, and choice. And we are spirits, designed to live in fellowship with God.

On that day, the spirit died. The lifeline was severed. Adam and Eve still walked and breathed, yet inside they were cut off from the very source of life. Though their bodies continued, the countdown had begun—the slow return to dust. Humanity died that day, just as God had said.

The effects were devastating. Every part of existence—spiritual, physical, relational, and even creation itself—fell under the shadow of death. Lucifer was cursed. Adam and Eve were cursed. The ground was cursed. Humanity was driven from Eden, exiled from the Source of life.

Everything changed. Spiritual death displaced spiritual life.

Work shifted from joy to survival.

Freedom gave way to bondage.

Relationship turned to fear—then blame—then manipulation.

Adam, the first ruler of the earth, abdicated his throne. He lost the authority God had entrusted to him allowing it to be placed into the hands of the deceiver. From that point on, Satan would be known as the ruler of this world

The Corruption of Humanity

Humanity stood helpless—separated from God, enslaved under corrupt powers, and poisoned by sin—the brokenness we all carry. The paradise of Eden had become a wilderness of sorrow and decay.

Violence grew unchecked. Scripture records that "the earth was filled with corruption and violence."[7] Even spiritual beings crossed boundaries, worsening humanity's descent.

In His justice and mercy, God sent the flood. It was both judgment and reset, a sweeping act that covered the whole earth. Only Noah, his wife, and their sons with their wives survived to begin again. Yet even after the waters receded, rebellion still clung to the human heart.

The Rebellious Powers and Nations

As Noah's descendants multiplied across the earth, God commanded them to spread out and fill it. Instead, they gathered together and built The Tower of Babel, a monument to their own glory. Their unity was not in obedience but in rebellion. So God scattered them, confusing their language and dispersing them across world. At this point of dispersion, Scripture reveals that God disinherited the nations[8], placing them under the governance of lesser spiritual beings. These beings—originally intended to steward creation under God's authority—became corrupt. They exalted themselves, demanded worship, and enslaved humanity under deception.

A follower of God—a prophet named Daniel, later saw these rulers in his visions, describing these powerful beings as "princes" over Persia and Greece. Paul — another follower — described them as operating within a kind of parallel hierarchy in the unseen realm, which he called the "principalities and powers."[9] Through mankind's rebellion, a counterfeit spiritual order took shape. Humanity, already estranged from God, now lived under the dominion of these fallen angels—these "false gods", trapped in a system of lies and oppression.

The Results

Freedom into Slavery

Where mankind was once free—free to love, to create, to explore, and to live in perfect harmony with God and with creation—we now fell into slavery.

Adam had abdicated his throne. Humanity's first king unknowingly handed the authority God had entrusted to him over to the deceiver. From that moment on, Satan became "the ruler of this world."[10] The human race was transferred from the kingdom of light into the domain of darkness, from children of God to children of wrath.

Death unfolded in layers. Spiritually, humanity was cut off from God—alive in body, yet dead at the core of our being. Physically, our bodies began to decay, each breath drawing us closer to the dust. In the soul, our thoughts and desires turned inward, binding us to fear, pride, and selfish ambition.

Humanity became enslaved in two ways:

First, we became slaves to a counterfeit world system. Cut off from God, we were drawn into a structure that Scripture describes as "the lust of the flesh, the lust of the eyes, and the pride of life."[11] It is the pursuit of gold, pleasure, and glory—whatever feeds the hunger of self. This is the system into which every person is born—broken people living in a broken world under broken rulers.

Second, we became slaves to our own desires. Severed from the true Source of life, we grew desperate for meaning and belonging. We sought safety, love, and purpose in the very system that enslaved us. The deceiver's promises of fulfillment only deepened our captivity. Humanity became addicted to a finite world, trying to fill the infinite emptiness left by separation from God.

Humanity's Lost Mission

Humanity's mission to rule, cultivate, and preserve creation was twisted into domination, exploitation, and endless striving. The image of stewardship gave way to self-centered control. What God designed for harmony became a contest for survival.

By rebellion's end, the picture was bleak:

• Humanity unplugged from God.

• Creation scarred and groaning.

• The spiritual realm fractured.

• Satan ruling as the prince of this world.

What began as paradise became a battlefield. Every longing, every ache, every injustice traces back to this moment. The fall was not merely a story of disobedience but of disconnection—the breaking of a divine relationship that once held all creation together in perfect order.

As this chapter closes, we are left with questions—about the flood, the age of the earth, and the nature of unseen powers. Each holds threads you can follow farther than these pages allow. For now, one truth remains unshakable—humanity left the garden hopeless and helpless to save itself.

Chapter 6

Broken Religions

Some Review

As the curtain closes on humanity's rebellion, we are left facing the wreckage of our condition. It is not that we simply made a mistake or stumbled into poor choices; our entire being has been twisted away from God. Scripture paints a sobering picture of where we now stand.

First, we are enslaved. We live under the dominion of the ruler of this world, bound to its system and to our own desires, unable to free ourselves.

Second, we are spiritually dead. Cut off from the source of life, we move and breathe, yet remain lifeless within. Our bodies function and our souls—our minds, wills, and emotions—continue to churn, but the spirit, meant for communion with God, lies dead.[1]

Third, we are legally guilty. Before a holy God, we stand condemned. Humanity has committed high treason against its rightful King and holds no defense or standing in His court.

Fourth, we are powerless. Even if we were to recognize our condition, we have no strength to alter it. We cannot lift ourselves to life or find our way back into the presence of God.

Finally, we have lost authority. Created to rule and care for God's world, we forfeited our stewardship. We surrendered our birthright and yielded dominion to another.

It is the human story after the fall—enslaved, dead, guilty, powerless, and dispossessed. Every religion, ritual, and system humanity has constructed since Babel has been an effort to climb out of this pit. Yet none of them can change the truth: we need more than repair—*we need rescue!*

Noah and his family came off the ark and began to resettle the earth. Within roughly 150 years after the flood, the population may have reached between forty and fifty thousand. It was then that the next great rebellion began. God had commanded humanity to be fruitful, multiply, and fill the earth, yet they chose defiance instead. Rather than spreading out, they remained together as one people and determined to build a tower "to reach the heavens."[2]

Once again, humanity sought heaven on its own terms. It was like a teenager stepping into adulthood—wanting freedom and independence, yet still craving safety and belonging. Humanity longed for autonomy from God while still desiring the benefits of His presence. They wanted a relationship without surrender, blessing without obedience. So they set out to build their tower to the heavens.

It was humanity's first organized religion, born out of pride and self-reliance. The project was destined to fail. No matter how tall or splendid the structure, it could *never* bridge the gap between earth and heaven. Human pride would only deepen the separation. United yet spiritually broken, humanity clung to a false sense of security in its own achievements—draining creation's resources, boasting in progress, and dying as they had lived: apart from God.

So God intervened. He confused their language, dividing them by families and clans, and scattered them across the earth.

The Nations

When God divided the nations, He gave the people what they had chosen—life apart from Him. Scripture reflects on this moment, explaining that God "fixed the borders of the peoples according to the number of the sons of God."[3] Seventy nations were formed, each placed under the oversight of supernatural beings, these rulers and authorities, who became their spiritual rulers.

But these rulers did not shepherd well. Instead of guiding the nations toward truth, they led them into corruption. The psalmist records God's rebuke of these spiritual rulers: "You are gods, sons of the Most High, all of you; nevertheless, like men you shall die, and fall like any prince."[4] They were meant to reflect divine justice and life, yet they fostered oppression, idolatry, and ruin.

Here, religion took root. Cut off from the living God, humanity turned to systems of doing—rituals, sacrifices, chants, and ceremonies—all attempts to reach or manipulate the divine. These efforts could not touch the real problem: humanity's spiritual death and separation from its Creator.

The result was tragic. Across civilizations, worship descended into acts that dehumanized the very people offering it:

1. Parents burned their children in fire to Molech.

2. Men and women prostituted themselves in temples, hoping fertility gods would bless their fields.

3. Cities were drenched in blood, as if cruelty itself could win favor with heaven.

Religion became a new form of bondage. What began as a search for connection became a cycle of fear, guilt, and superstition. People longed for life but sought it in the shadows. The nations walked in darkness, reaching for light where none could be found.

Israel's Story

Yet God did not abandon humanity. After Babel, as the nations turned toward lesser powers, God chose one man to begin a new story. His name was Abram—later changed to Abraham. Through him, God established a covenant that would one day bring redemption to all peoples. Abraham's son Isaac and grandson Jacob continued that line. Jacob's name was changed to Israel, and his descendants grew into the nation that bore his name.

The idea was simple yet radical: Israel was meant to be a living picture of what life with the true God looked like. They were not chosen because they were better or stronger than others. They were chosen so the world could see—through them—what it meant to belong to the Creator. Over time, however, Israel stumbled into the same traps as the nations around them. Even when they turned back to God, their repentance often hardened into ritual. Faith became a checklist, and worship became a performance.

Prophets rose to call them back to the heart of the covenant. They reminded Israel that what God desired was not empty ceremony, but a relationship rooted in love, humility, justice, and mercy. Yet again and again, the people traded relationship for religion.

In the end, Israel became a reflection of the nations they were meant to transform. Their story proved that no system of effort or ritual could fix the deeper issue: humanity was spiritually dead, cut off from the life of God.

The Current State of Religion

Since Babel, humanity has never stopped building religions. Whether under the idols of the nations or within Israel's own rituals, people have poured their energy into systems of doing—sacrifices, pilgrimages, prayers, offerings, and rules. Each promised a way to reach God, earn His favor, or appease unseen powers.

But none of these efforts touched the root problem. Humanity is not merely lost or confused; we are spiritually dead, severed from the source of life. Religion became our attempt to manage guilt through offerings, to silence fear through ritual, to prove devotion through performance. Yet all our striving comes back to the same truth—our spirit is lifeless, and no amount of "doing" can raise the dead.

Across the world, religions compete for allegiance, each claiming to hold the truth. Some emphasize morality, others meditation or ritual, and still others strict obedience to law. Yet whether ancient or modern, they all share the same flaw: every system redirects the focus toward human effort. They assume the problem lies in ignorance, poor behavior, or lack of devotion, and then prescribe solutions we can perform through our own strength.

Scripture diagnoses something deeper. We are not merely misinformed or misguided; we are enslaved, guilty, powerless, and spiritually dead. Religion cannot heal that condition because it only tells us what to do. And "doing" is never enough when the real problem is who we are.

Illustration: Dogs and Cats

Consider a simple illustration. Imagine, for the sake of explanation, that God possesses a cat-like nature. Adam and Eve, created in His image, shared that same nature. It made them compatible with God and able to dwell in His presence. They were not divine themselves, but they reflected His character.

When they fell, that likeness was corrupted. Their nature changed. In this illustration, they became more like dogs than cats. No longer compatible with God, they passed on that altered nature to their descendants. Adam and Eve did not have kittens; they had puppies. Every generation since has been born spiritually dead.

In this picture, those with a cat-like nature do what comes naturally to them—they "meow," which represents goodness flowing from God's own nature. Those with a dog-like nature "bark," and in this analogy, barking symbolizes sin.

Here's where religion enters the picture. Religion fails because most of what it tries to do is teach dogs how to meow. It builds systems of behavior, training programs, rituals, and rules designed to make people act the way they believe God desires. But the problem is not that we bark instead of meow; the problem is that we are dogs. The issue is not our behavior but our nature. We do not need to learn how to meow. We need to become something new.

Imagine someone standing before God at the end of their life, proudly saying, "Listen to how well I meow." God might answer, "You meow beautifully. But the problem is, you are still a dog." The issue is not simply our sins—our barking—but rather who we are on the inside.

Religion cannot change that. Training, rules, and rituals cannot give life to what is dead. What humanity needs is not moral improvement but a new beginning. If only there could be a second Adam—one who could restore what was lost.

Chapter 7

Promises

Let's Review Our Dilemma

The world is a mess. You do not need a degree in theology or philosophy to see it. Headlines scream of violence, corruption, injustice, and despair. People are hurting, afraid, and deeply divided. But this is not merely a series of unfortunate events. It is a symptom of something deeper: a fundamental fracture in the created order.

This brokenness is not only external—it resides within us. Humanity, created to reflect the image of God and to steward the world, has become corrupted and severed from its source of life. We forfeited our role, rebelled against our Maker, and now stagger under the weight of guilt, confusion, and spiritual disconnection.

This is not simply a failure of morals. It is a rebellion with eternal consequences. We chose sides—against the One who made us. This is not just bad behavior. It is cosmic treason.

And here is the most sobering reality: we cannot fix it ourselves. Not with politics, technology, or even religion. We stand guilty before a just God. Even our most noble intentions fall short. Our hearts are twisted, our judgment clouded, and justice—true justice—demands that the consequence match the crime. As we have said before, love requires choice. Choice brings consequence. Justice demands that the consequence be just. That truth cannot be ignored. A debt remains. Payment is due.

God Disinherits the Nations

We have seen that after humanity's united rebellion at Babel, God responded by giving the nations what they insisted on: autonomy. God disinherited the nations, assigning them to lesser spiritual beings. In this act, He essentially declared, "If you will not follow me, then go your own way."

The implications were enormous. The world became not only fractured but also placed under the governance of lesser spiritual rulers—beings who, in time, became corrupted themselves. Scripture portrays a divine courtroom scene where God calls these rulers to account, declaring that they have failed in justice and will fall like any mortal.

Yet even as God handed the nations over, He reserved one portion for Himself. Israel became His inheritance—His chosen people. Not because they were greater or more deserving, but because He had a plan. A revealed plan: to form a people of promise. And a hidden one, though written across the pages of Scripture—to reclaim what had been lost.

Man's Failed Attempts at Religion

Even in rebellion, humanity has never stopped trying to rebuild Eden—Heaven on Earth. From ancient altars to modern moral frameworks, we have crafted systems to justify ourselves, soothe our guilt, and mend what is broken. But they fail.

Human religion and moral order repeat the same mistake: modification without transformation. We polish the surface while the heart decays. We build temples, draft laws, and make sacrifices, yet we cannot erase guilt, restore relationships, or breathe life into what has died within us.

Trying to heal humanity through religion or any man-made institution is like stitching a wound with spider webs. It might look intricate—even beautiful—but it cannot mend what is torn. Something greater is required. Something deeper. Something divine.

But God Promised...

In the midst of failure and judgment, God spoke hope. His promises were not vague or abstract. They were specific, unfolding step by step through history—each one pointing forward to the One who would set everything right.

The Promise in the Garden

Right there, in the aftermath of humanity's fall, God spoke directly to the serpent with a mysterious but powerful prophecy: "He shall bruise your head, and you shall bruise his heel."[1] It was the first whisper of redemption. A "seed" from the woman would come—a human descendant—who would crush the serpent's power, even though the victory would come at great cost.

This was a promise of triumph through suffering, a declaration that the serpent's dominion would not last forever.

The Covenant with Abraham

Not long after humanity's rebellion at Babel, God called a man named Abram to leave his homeland and journey to a place that God Himself would give him. There, God made three promises: land, a seed, and blessing for all the families of the earth. In time, Abram became Abraham, the father of Isaac, whose son Jacob would become the father of twelve sons—the ancestors of the nation of Israel.

But this covenant was about more than the birth of a nation. The word "seed" carried a deeper meaning. It pointed not only to a people but to a singular descendant—a coming one through whom God would reclaim the nations. The promise was always outward, always redemptive. What had been broken in Eden would one day be healed through this covenant line.

The Covenant with David

About a thousand years later, God made another covenant—this time with King David. He promised that one of David's descendants would reign forever.[2] His kingdom would be marked by righteousness, justice, and peace that no power could overthrow.

The prophet Isaiah later described this reign with breathtaking imagery: wolves dwelling beside lambs, lions eating straw like oxen, and the earth filled with the knowledge of the Lord as the waters cover the sea.[3] It was a vision of restored creation, a world where God's rule would bring harmony once more.

This would not be an ordinary king. He would reclaim not only Israel's throne, but every throne—uniting heaven and earth under His eternal rule.

The Vision of Daniel

Centuries later, during Israel's exile, God gave the prophet Daniel a striking vision. He saw "one like a son of man" coming with the clouds of heaven.[4] This figure—the Son of Man—was given dominion, glory, and a kingdom that would never end.

Here, the promise narrowed to a single person, a coming ruler whose authority would be both divine and eternal. He was human, yet more than human—one who could stand before God—the Ancient of Days—and receive everlasting power. Could this be the Second Adam? The one who would reclaim the authority humanity lost and rule where the first Adam failed?

The Global Declaration

Even in the midst of Israel's rebellion, God spoke again, this time making an oath by His own name: "As surely as I live, all the earth shall be filled with the glory of the Lord."[5]

This was not a vague wish. It was a cosmic declaration—a vision of total renewal. The curse would be undone, creation restored, and justice, peace, and life would once again flow freely through the world. What began as a garden would end as a kingdom filled with God's presence, His glory covering the earth as water covers the sea.

The Shape of the Promise

From the garden to the nations, from a single family to a chosen King, the thread of promise has been tightening. And now, it begins to widen again.

It was never Plan B. This was the plan from the beginning.

Through these promises, God was not merely offering comfort. He was revealing His plan for justice, mercy, and redemption. Each covenant pointed forward, preparing the way for the fulfillment of every promise.

But these covenants were not only about kings and nations. They were also deeply personal. Each one involved flawed yet faithful individuals—Abraham, Isaac, Jacob, Daniel, and David—men who, despite weakness and failure, believed.

Their faith mattered. Where Adam and Eve doubted, they trusted. Their trust in God's promises pleased Him in a way nothing else could. They were still broken, still bound by the same fallen nature. Yet their faith in what God would do was counted to them as "being made right with God". It was a belief that bridged the gap, a belief that drew them into the unfolding plan of redemption.

God's Unfolding Promise

God had made promises—real, specific, and binding. He had chosen a people, revealed a plan, and pointed to a coming King. Through it all, a pattern emerged: those who believed Him were counted as "right" with Him. Not because they were perfect. Not because they were powerful. But because they believed.

Even so, the world remained fractured. The curse lingered. Evil still held sway. The promises had been spoken, but not yet fulfilled. Hope had been planted, yet the harvest was still to come.

Something more was coming. Something greater. But before fulfillment could arrive, the world had to be prepared. The stage had to be set.

And so, in the silence between the promises and their fulfillment, God continued to work—quietly, faithfully, sovereignly—shaping history toward redemption.

Chapter 8

In the Fullness of Time . . .

Have you ever watched one of those Mission Impossible movies where the plan seems to fall apart in every direction? The team's scattered, the mission's compromised, and the whole thing looks doomed. Then, at the very last moment, it all snaps together—every twist, every setback, every impossible turn somehow fits perfectly into place. You realize the chaos wasn't chaos at all. It was choreography.

That's what this chapter is about. History looked out of control—empires rising and falling, languages changing, nations scattering and reforming. But behind it all, something intentional was unfolding. Every movement, every moment, was leading toward a single point in time when heaven's plan would intersect with earth's story. A first century writer would later describe it with four simple words: "In the fullness of time."

I hope by now you see that this is not simply another reflection on religion or speculation about the unseen. This is a history of the world—the true story of God's creative purpose, His desire for both a spiritual and human family, and the astonishing lengths He has gone to bring that purpose to pass in a world where people are free to choose where they place their love and loyalty.

Israel's story stands at the center of that history. God did not choose them because they were strong or numerous, but because through them He intended to bless every nation. We left off with David, the king after God's own heart, and with the promise of a son who would reign on his throne forever. But after David came Solomon—his wisdom great, his kingdom glorious, yet his devotion divided. The nation followed his pattern. Division came, then decline. Israel turned from the living God to the false gods of the surrounding nations. It wasn't long before the fallout came—enemies rose, prophets warned, judgment came.

By the time the Babylonian Empire appeared on the horizon, Israel was fractured, vulnerable, and spiritually adrift. Yet even in judgment, God was not absent. His promises still held, unbroken. But before they could find their fulfillment, foreign powers would trample Israel's soil again and again.

The Crossroads of the World

The land of Israel has never been easy ground. From a human perspective, it sat at the center of everything. To the east rose the great empires of Mesopotamia—Assyria, Babylon, and Persia. To the southwest stood Egypt, ancient and enduring. To the north lay Anatolia and, in time, Greece. And to the west stretched the Mediterranean—a doorway to distant lands and cultures.

Whoever controlled this narrow strip of earth controlled the trade routes that stitched the ancient world together. That meant armies were always moving—passing through, fighting over, or occupying the land. Israel was a crossroads—and crossroads rarely know peace.[1]

Yet there was more to it than geopolitics. Scripture reveals that the struggle over Israel was also spiritual. From the Tower of Babel onward, the nations were divided under the authority of rebellious spiritual powers, while God claimed Israel as His own inheritance.[2] To the unseen rulers of the nations, Israel represented a threat—the one people through whom God had promised to bless the whole world. Time after time, their story carried undertones of attempted eradication: Pharaoh in Egypt's slavery, Amalek in the wilderness, Haman in Persia's courts, Antiochus in Jerusalem's temple. Each effort echoed the same dark strategy: destroy God's people, and you cut off God's plan.

So Israel's history cannot be read as merely the story of a small nation caught between superpowers. It was that, but it was also far more. It became the stage on which the conflict between God and the rebellious powers of heaven was played out. Every empire that rose to prominence found itself drawn into this struggle—often without realizing it.

Babylon (c. 605–539 BC) – Israel in Exile

When Babylon's armies stormed Jerusalem, the fall was more than political—it was theological. The temple burned, the king was blinded, and the people were led away in chains. In the imagination of the ancient world, such a defeat meant that your god had been defeated as well. To all who watched, it appeared that Marduk, the god of Babylon, had triumphed over Yahweh—the God of Israel—on His own sacred ground.

Exile was more than the loss of freedom. In the ancient mind, gods were tied to specific places. To be removed from your land was to be torn from your god. That is why Babylon not only conquered nations but also deported them. By removing a people from their homeland, they believed they were severing that people's bond with their deity.[3]

For Israel, the wound cut even deeper. Their Scriptures taught that, after Babel, God had assigned the nations to lesser spiritual beings while reserving Israel as His own inheritance. The land of Israel was Yahweh's portion—the place where His name dwelt. To be torn from it and made to live under the shadow of foreign gods in a foreign land felt like abandonment, as though they had been exiled not only from home but from God Himself.

The exile was not uniform. Not every Israelite was carried away to Babylon. Some remained in the land under foreign rule, while others were scattered throughout the empire—to Egypt, Mesopotamia, and beyond. Many never returned, even when the opportunity arose. They became the first seeds of a Jewish diaspora that would stretch across the Mediterranean world—faithful pockets of God's people living outside His chosen portion.[4]

By the rivers of Babylon we sat and wept—because in a foreign land, the Lord's song would not come.[5] Their identity as God's chosen people seemed to fade like a memory lost in the smoke of a ruined city.

Yet exile transformed them. With no temple to gather around, they formed new rhythms of worship. They met in synagogues, clung to the Scriptures, and prayed toward a home that seemed impossibly far away. Prophets such as Jeremiah and Ezekiel insisted that exile was not divine defeat but divine discipline. They declared that God Himself had sent His people away and would one day bring them back.[7]

But Babylon's splendor was brief. Within decades, the armies of Persia under Cyrus swept into Babylon without resistance, and a new chapter began.[6]

Persia (c. 539–331 BC) – Cyrus the Champion

Conquerors were rarely known for compassion. The usual method was to scatter the defeated, suppress their identity, and erase every trace of their culture. Yet Cyrus of Persia did something unexpected.

Cyrus proclaimed, "The Lord, the God of heaven, has given me all the kingdoms of the earth, and He has appointed me to build Him a house in Jerusalem..."[7]

Cyrus not only allowed the Jews to return home but also ordered the rebuilding of the temple and restored the sacred vessels that Babylon had taken. For Israel, this was more than political relief—it was a shock of hope.

Nonbiblical evidence tells the same story. The Cyrus Cylinder, discovered in Babylon and now kept in the British Museum, records how Cyrus returned displaced peoples to their homelands and supported the restoration of their temples.[8] To the world, this was shrewd diplomacy. To Israel, it was divine intervention. Their God was not bound to one land or temple. He directed kings and empires to fulfill His purpose.

Yet even this restoration was partial. The people had a temple but no king on David's throne. They were back in the land, but not in the glory they remembered. Persia gave them a glimpse of renewal, but more than that, it prepared the way for what was still to come.

Persia's strength, however, soon waned. From the west, a young Macedonian commander named Alexander swept across the ancient world, carrying with him not only conquest but a culture that would reshape civilization itself.

Greece (c. 331–167 BC) – Alexander's Common World

When Alexander the Great surged across the known world, he did more than defeat Persia. He forged a new kind of empire. In every city he founded, he left behind Greek culture—its theaters, marketplaces, schools, and above all, its language.[9]

This Koine Greek became the common language from Egypt to Mesopotamia. Centuries later, it would be the very language in which Israel's Scriptures were translated—the Septuagint—making the words of the prophets accessible not only to Jews but to anyone who could read Greek.[10]

Greek thought also left its mark. Philosophers sought to uncover the order behind the universe. Some called it the Logos—the rational principle, the reason, the word that held all things together.[11] The Stoics spoke of the Logos as the divine spark within creation, the pattern woven through all existence. In Alexandria, Jewish thinkers began blending Hebrew revelation with Greek reasoning, describing God's wisdom as His Logos—His Word active within the world.[12]

It was a compelling idea, but also a restless one. Humanity longed for meaning that was not myth, for truth that could anchor the soul. Greece gave the world both a shared language and a shared question: *What is the Logos that holds everything together?*

Yet Greek culture also carried a sharper edge. For many rulers, "Hellenization" meant more than language and art—it meant conformity. And nowhere did that clash erupt more fiercely than in Judea, under the Seleucid kings.

The Seleucids and the Maccabean Revolt (c. 175–160 BC) – A Taste of Deliverance

Greek influence did not stop with ideas. After Alexander's death, his empire was divided, and in time the Seleucid kings came to rule Judea. They pushed for more than political loyalty. The goal was cultural absorption: shared gods, shared customs, shared identity. At first, the changes came quietly—gymnasiums, theaters, Greek names.

But under Antiochus IV Epiphanes—a Seleucid ruler obsessed with unifying his empire under Greek culture and divine kingship—it became violent.

Antiochus outlawed Sabbath observance, circumcision, and devotion to God's law. Anyone caught honoring the covenant faced death. He desecrated the temple by dedicating it to Zeus and offering unclean sacrifices upon its altar.[13] For faithful Jews, it was the unthinkable: the holy dwelling place of God transformed into a shrine for idols.

The trauma ran deep. Parents watched their children executed for refusing to abandon their devotion. Elders were slaughtered for declining to eat forbidden food. The Books of the Maccabees tell of entire families martyred rather than betray their God.[14] Antiochus Epiphanes became, in Jewish memory, the embodiment of blasphemy—the prototype of the ultimate tyrant who would rise against God and His people.

Out of persecution came resistance. A priestly family, the Hasmoneans, rose in defiance. Led first by the priest Mattathias and then by his son Judas Maccabeus—"the Hammer"—they fought against impossible odds, driving out Seleucid forces and reclaiming Jerusalem. In 164 BC, they cleansed and rededicated the temple, an event still commemorated at Hanukkah.[15]

For a brief generation, Israel tasted independence again. The Hasmonean dynasty ruled Judea as both priests and kings, yet power soon corrupted them. Their internal rivalries and moral compromises weakened the nation from within. Hope for lasting renewal faded, and the people's longing deepened—for a deliverer greater than Judas Maccabeus, one who could restore not only the temple but the world itself. The Hasmonean line collapsed, and by 63 BC, Rome marched into Jerusalem and took control. To many Jews, Daniel's visions seemed to be unfolding before their eyes. If Rome was the fourth kingdom, then God's kingdom must be near.

Daniel's Vision of the Kingdoms

While living as an exile in Babylon, the prophet Daniel saw a vision of a massive statue—its head made of gold, its chest and arms of silver, its middle of bronze, and its legs of iron. Each part represented a kingdom that would rise and then fall, one after another, until a final kingdom from God struck the statue like a stone, shattering it completely and growing into a mountain that filled the whole earth.

Later, Daniel saw another vision describing the same story in a different way: four beasts rising from the sea, each more terrifying than the one before. These beasts mirrored the metals of the statue—earthly empires rising in power, devouring and dominating, until one "like a Son of Man" came with the authority of heaven and received an everlasting kingdom from God.[16]

By the first century, Jewish interpreters believed that three of those empires—Babylon, Persia, and Greece—had already passed. The fourth, Rome, now ruled the world. If their reading were correct, the next kingdom to appear would be the kingdom of God. What they could not yet see was that Daniel's vision had not fully played out. History was still advancing towards its ultimate fulfillment. And, who was this Son of Man?

Rome (c. 63 BC–AD 70) – The Iron Kingdom

Rome marched into Jerusalem in 63 BC under Pompey the Great, and everything changed. From that day forward, Israel was no longer its own. Roman soldiers patrolled the streets, governors ruled in Caesar's name, and taxes drained the land into foreign treasuries. To some, Rome brought order—roads, law, and the kind of peace that came only through fear. To most Jews, Rome brought humiliation and grief.

Through the visions of Daniel, many saw Rome as the iron kingdom—the fourth empire, strong as iron, crushing and devouring all in its path. Babylon had fallen. Persia had fallen. Greece had fallen. Now Rome held the world in its grasp, and if Daniel's prophecy were true, the next kingdom to rise would be God's.

The mood was tense. Different groups responded in different ways:

- The Pharisees, a movement of religious purists, clung fiercely to ritual and moral purity, convinced that scrupulous devotion to God's law could keep Israel distinct until deliverance came.

- The Sadducees, the priestly and political elite, sought compromise—aligning themselves with Roman power to maintain control over the temple and preserve their status.

- The Essenes, a separatist community of mystics and reformers, retreated into the wilderness, waiting for God to bring judgment on the corrupt order.

- The Zealots, militant nationalists driven by passion for freedom, sharpened their blades, ready to rise in revolt.

All were waiting—in their own way—for God to break Rome's hold.

For the ordinary Jew walking the streets of Jerusalem, life under Rome was a mixture of oppression and expectation. The weight of foreign rule was heavy, yet the promises of Scripture burned with hope. If Rome were the iron kingdom, then the next reign would not belong to any man. The world was restless, fractured, and ready for something greater.

Chapter Conclusion

Empire after empire had risen and fallen. Babylon scarred Israel with exile and scattering. Persia offered a glimpse of restoration but left David's throne empty. Greece united the world through a common language and a shared hunger for meaning. The Seleucids traumatized Israel with persecution but awakened fierce devotion and the memory of revolt. Then came Rome, pressing down with iron strength, while the people lived with the conviction that they were standing in the final days before God's reign would break in. They had a model of resistance from the Maccabees and a deep longing for redemption. It was the perfect storm—politically, culturally, and spiritually.

The nations were bound together by language and roads, yet divided by pride and power. Israel was scattered across the world, yet more determined than ever to cling to its God. The stage was set. History itself seemed to hold its breath. The world could wait no longer.

And so here we are—the unfolding of a hidden plan conceived before time began. The faithful sensed something approaching. Even wise men far beyond Israel's borders saw faint signs of it. But no one saw *this* coming.

None of it was coincidence. The languages, the roads, the philosophies, even the restless longing of the human heart—all of it had been moving toward this. What looked like history's chaos was, in truth, choreography. Every empire that rose and fell, every exile, every reform, every silence between the prophets—all of it was part of a plan written long before the world began. And when the curtain lifted, the moment finally arrived. Heaven's mission was not impossible at all. It was unfolding exactly as designed.

Recall earlier we considered the Greek idea of the Logos. In modern English, it translates simply as Word—a plain word, yet one carrying immense weight. To the Greek mind, Logos was the defining principle of reality, the order that connected all things. But no one imagined that this Logos—this Defining Principle—would take on flesh, enter history, and change the world forever.

This is how that Logos—that Word was described:

From the very beginning, the Word already existed. He was with God in the most intimate fellowship, and He was God in His very nature. And then the unimaginable happened: the Word became flesh and dwelt among us, and we beheld His glory.[17]

In the fullness of time . . . God sent His Son.

Chapter 9

Return of the King, Part 1

Setting the Stage

For centuries, the people of Israel had lived in the tension between promise and silence. They held to the hope of a coming rescuer—one who would set things right, deliver them from oppression, and restore the glory of their nation. They even had a title for him—Messiah—a divinely anointed and appointed deliverer.

But time wore on. Empire after empire claimed their land: Babylon, Persia, Greece, and now Rome. The prophets' voices had faded, and generations had come and gone without a word. Hope remained, but it trembled on the edge of despair.

Yet the expectation endured. When the Messiah arrived, He would be a warrior-king—a leader like David, the poet and conqueror who united Israel under God's banner. God had promised David that one of his descendants would reign on his throne forever.

So they imagined a new David. A king who would rise, overthrow Rome, and bring peace back to Israel.

The stage was set. The longing was fierce. And then, without warning, the story took a turn no one could have foreseen.

A Warrior After All — Just Not the Enemy They Expected

In a quiet village called Bethlehem—the same town where David had been born centuries before—a child entered the world. Bethlehem lay only a short journey from Jerusalem, no more than a two-hour walk. The family later moved north to Nazareth, a tiny settlement nearly a week's journey away.

Bethlehem was scarcely more than a village, and Nazareth even less. So obscure was Nazareth that it is absent from the Old Testament and nearly all ancient records.[1] Yet from these forgotten places came the King of all creation. The world expected deliverance from marble halls and royal courts. Instead, it came wrapped in the simplicity of an ordinary birth.

This boy, raised in obscurity, grew into a man filled with wisdom and purpose. Around the age of thirty, He began to travel through the towns of Galilee, teaching, healing, and drawing a growing crowd of followers. His name was Jesus.

If your idea of Jesus comes from cultural leftovers—paintings of a pale man, seasonal slogans, or a cross worn as jewelry—you probably do not know Him at all. Most of what passes for common knowledge about Jesus is more myth than truth.

He was not a wandering teacher who became a casualty of history. He was not a crutch for the fearful or the weak. He was God's final Word—the living revelation of truth, life, and love. He was, and is, the way back to heaven.

Jesus is the Logos—the Word. His is the image hidden in the stereogram, the reality behind every shadow.

He did not come to create another religion. Religion, as we know it can train, refine, and reform, but it cannot transform. Jesus came to heal our brokenness, to restore the divine image twisted by being severed from the Source of life. He came to make us new, to turn us from lost creatures into true image bearers of God.

For centuries, Israel had longed for a deliverer. Their Scriptures foretold a king who would rise from David's line, bring justice, and reestablish God's reign on earth. The people expected a warrior who would overthrow Caesar, drive out Rome, and restore Israel's independence.

What they received was something far greater—not what they imagined, but exactly what they needed.

The Trinity entered history. The Father sent. The Son came. The Spirit empowered. Jesus, the Son—God Himself, crossed enemy lines in the one way the powers of darkness never anticipated—by taking on human flesh.

This was no mere footnote in history. It was an invasion. The seed of the woman, promised long ago, had arrived.

In Jesus, the divine and human were joined in one person.

Born of a virgin, He was fully man—able to stand in our place. He had to be. The first Adam abandoned his calling. Only another Adam—guiltless and untouched by the authority of Satan—could take it back.

But He was also fully God. He had to be. If He were only a finite man, His act could have redeemed Adam alone. But as the infinite One, the great I AM, He could redeem the entire human race. Without being both, the rescue of humanity would have been impossible.

Yes, the King arrived, though not as Israel expected, and not as the powers of darkness desired. The seed of the woman was God Himself. His coming shook both earth and hell.

The people expected a warrior-king to crush Rome. They got one—but His battlefield was far greater, and His enemy far older than the Roman Empire.

The King Reveals Himself

When Jesus stepped into public life, He entered the temple—the heart of Israel's worship—and drove out the merchants and money changers who had turned prayer into profit.

This was no impulsive act of rage. It was a declaration: the King was reclaiming His Father's house.

To the crowds, it may have echoed the memory of Judas Maccabeus, the priest-warrior who once cleansed the temple from pagan defilement. To the unseen powers of darkness, it was the sound of war.

The leaders were outraged. The people were stirred. Yet he did not form an army, raise taxes, or forge weapons. Instead, He proclaimed good news to people experiencing poverty. He healed the sick, opened blind eyes, and called the dead to life.

People began to whisper, "Who is this man?"

The signs He performed were never for spectacle. Each miracle was proof that He was the promised one and a preview of the world to come—a world where sickness, hunger, and death would no longer reign.

Every healing was like a glimpse through the veil, a short trailer of the Kingdom breaking into the present.

Rising Tension—Leaders and People Respond

Not everyone welcomed Him.

The religious leaders saw their power slipping away. The political rulers feared unrest. Rome tolerated no rivals. Any rumor of a king—any king—was dangerous.

Even the ordinary people began to waver. At first, the miracles filled them with hope. Perhaps this was the one they had been waiting for. But when He refused to raise an army or take up arms, disappointment grew.

Jesus was clearly on a mission, but not the kind they wanted. They longed for revolt. He came for redemption. They wanted Rome defeated. He came to conquer death itself.

He did not fit their expectations. He did not fit their categories. To many, He became just another failed hope.

What Did Jesus Come to Conquer?

Israel believed their true enemy was Rome. But Rome was only a symptom. The real enemies were far older: sin, death, and Satan.

From the beginning, a shadow had fallen over humanity—the curse of Eden. Yet the ancient promise remained: one day, a child of the woman would crush the serpent's head. That day had come.

Before the final confrontation, the battles had already begun. In the desert, that same adversary that tempted Eve came again, offering shortcuts: bread from stones, fame from spectacle, kingdoms in exchange for a bow. They were the same temptations he had used in Eden—food, beauty, and power.

In the beginning, Adam and Eve chose to trust the serpent instead of God. In the desert, the story was reversed. Jesus chose to trust the Father's words. Every temptation was met with "It is written." Where Adam failed, Jesus prevailed.

From that point on, every step of His ministry became an act of war. What seemed like a teacher and His followers moving from village to village was, in truth, a campaign against the powers of darkness. The nations once handed over to fallen spiritual rulers were being reclaimed by the true King.

The conflict began with the temptation in the desert. Jesus made it known that He—the second Adam—was faithful, the rightful heir to the throne.

He silenced spirits that had tormented people, entered territories long held by dark forces, and revealed His glory at the mountain once tied to cosmic rebellion. With each act, He was taking back what had been lost—the hearts of humanity.

The campaign was in motion. The prince of this world was under attack. The gates of the adversary could not hold, and his house was being plundered.

But the decisive battle would not unfold in foreign lands or temple courts. It would take place on a hill outside Jerusalem.

The Great Showdown

The earthly leaders were desperate. The crowds seethed with anger. Under pressure, the Roman authorities yielded, and Jesus was condemned to death. The final confrontation unfolded at Golgotha—the "place of the skull." To those watching, it appeared to be the end. The King hung on a cross, broken and bleeding. His enemies celebrated. His followers fled. To the unseen realm, it seemed as though Satan had triumphed.

Did Satan truly want Jesus dead, or did he hope the Son would falter at the brink? Scripture leaves the question open. What it does reveal is that the powers of darkness completely misread the moment.

Just before His final breath, Jesus declared, "It is finished."[2] He wasn't surrendering His life; He was announcing victory. In Greek, the phrase was a legal and financial term, stamped on receipts to signify that a debt had been canceled. The debt of sin—stretching all the way back to Adam—was now marked: paid in full.

The curse that began in Eden[6] met its undoing at Golgotha. His heel was bruised, but in that bruising, the serpent's head was crushed. Even in death, Jesus, the second Adam trusted the Father. The curse had met its match.

Death and Resurrection—The Second Adam

But how could death be victory? How could the defeated become the conqueror?

According to Scripture, Jesus' body was laid in a tomb, sealed with a massive stone so no one could claim He had risen. On the first day of the week, a group of women—His followers—came to the tomb and found the stone rolled away. Two angels stood there and asked, "Why are you looking for the living among the dead? He is not here, but has risen."[3]

He walked out alive. The stone rolled away. The grave was left empty. Death, at last, was defeated at its own game.

C. S. Lewis captured the essence of this mystery in his allegory *The Lion, the Witch, and the Wardrobe*. The White Witch appeals to the "Deep Magic from the dawn of time," a law declaring that every traitor belongs to her and must die. When Aslan (the Lion, symbolizing Jesus) dies in the place of a traitor, she believes she has won. But Aslan reveals a "Deeper Magic from before the dawn of time," a greater law that declares: if a willing, innocent victim offers himself for a traitor, death itself will begin to work backward.[4]

The first man, Adam, brought sin and death. The second Adam, Jesus, brought righteousness—and now death itself has begun to unravel.

What the Resurrection Accomplished

That victory changed everything.

The guilty are no longer condemned; the debt is paid.

The Accuser has lost his claim; the rightful King has reclaimed the throne.

The enslaved are no longer bound; their master's power is broken.

The spiritually dead live again; the connection to God is restored.

Physical death is no longer the end; it has become a doorway.

Those who once walked in darkness now walk in light; a new Kingdom has begun.

Every ancient promise found its "Yes" in Him[5]—the blessing given to Abraham, the throne promised to David, and the long-awaited hope of the prophets. All of it converged in one Person, in one moment.

Now What?

We've come full circle. Love is only love when it is chosen, and choice always carries consequences. Adam chose, and we inherited his fall. Jesus chose, and we can inherit His victory.

Now we face the same choice Adam did. We can go our own way, or we can place our trust in God. Like Abraham, Isaac, Jacob, David, and all who followed them in faith, we can choose to believe—to believe in what God has done. We owed a debt we could not pay, and He paid a debt He did not owe. If we place our faith in that truth, with no Plan B, we inherit the new life He reclaimed. The price has been paid. Now we can choose, and this time, we can win where Adam failed.

Religion focuses primarily on behavior—a surface attempt to fix what is broken inside. But Jesus, the second Adam, brings transformation. Those who trust in Him become new creations, remade from the inside out.

What will you choose? Each of us must decide. God does not force love. He honors our freedom. We can live for eternity apart from Him—cut off from the Source of life—or we can be reunited with our Creator and share in the glory of the Return of Heaven.

The Kingdom has begun, but it is not yet complete. The decisive victory has been won, yet the final chapter is still to come.

Israel was not entirely wrong about their Messiah. They simply misunderstood the timing. The King will come again, and when He does, He will reign as the Last Adam, setting all things right.

But before that day arrives, one more mystery unfolds—a story that begins with a wedding to be prepared.

Chapter 10

The Great Invitation

Why the Cross Works

If Chapter 9 declared the victory, this section explains why it truly works. How can one act—one man's death and resurrection—alter the course of all creation? The Bible answers with six sweeping truths.

The debt is paid.

We inherited Adam's brokenness—not merely guilt, but a heart that stopped trusting God. That failure passed to every generation, leaving behind a debt of rebellion too great for any human to pay. Justice required that a man cover the cost, yet no guilty man could do it for another. Only an innocent one could stand in our place, and only God could make the payment large enough for everyone. In Jesus—fully human and fully divine—both conditions were met. The debt was cleared forever.

The throne is reclaimed.

Adam was meant to rule beneath God's authority, but when he yielded to the serpent, he broke allegiance and surrendered the dominion entrusted to him. Satan seized what was not his and claimed the crown. Jesus came as the second Adam, facing the same test. Where Adam failed, Jesus remained faithful, even unto death. Because He stood firm, the usurper's claim was broken. The throne that was lost has been restored.

The chains are broken.

Every person knows the feeling of being trapped—habits that bind, guilt that echoes, shame that will not quiet down. That is what it means to live enslaved to a fallen nature. At the cross, Jesus shattered the lock. The chains may still rattle, but they no longer rule. Old habits die hard, and temptation still whispers, but its power is gone. We are free.

The spirit is reborn.

We were not merely sick inside; we were spiritually lifeless. Separated from the Source of life, our spirits were dead. Dead things cannot revive themselves. Through Jesus, God breathes life once more into what was lost. Our spirit is reborn and reconnected to Him. Through the resurrection, when we choose to trust in Jesus rather than ourselves, our dead spirit arises with a new nature—the God-connected life that was meant to be ours from the beginning.

Death is defeated.

The true sting of death is not the ceasing of breath but the eternal separation from God. That was the destiny set in motion by Adam's fall. Yet Jesus entered death and emerged alive. Through Him, death has lost its power. For all who place their trust in Him, death no longer signifies endless separation; it becomes a passage into genuine life—eternal life.

Our citizenship has changed.

Adam's rebellion placed humanity under a false ruler, what Scripture calls the "domain of darkness."[1] But through His victory, Jesus reclaimed us. We have been transferred into God's family, brought under His reign within the kingdom of light.[2] A new realm has dawned, and we are invited to live within it.

These truths are not distant or theoretical. They embody the Logos—the divine logic that orders all creation and gives meaning to existence. The depth of its internal logic explains why one moment in history possesses the power to redefine every other moment—for anyone willing to wrestle with it.

Our Response

As we've learned, love is only genuine when it is freely chosen, and every choice brings consequences. Adam chose rebellion, and humanity inherited his fall. Jesus chose obedience, and through Him, we can share in His victory. Now the decision rests with us.

We can follow our own path, or we can trust completely in what God has accomplished. We owed a debt we could never repay, yet He paid a debt He never owed. When we place our full confidence in that truth, with no backup plan, we receive the new life He restored.

Religion focuses on changing behavior, but that cannot heal the heart. Jesus, the second Adam, offers true transformation. When we surrender to Him, we are made new.

"Desperado, why don't you come to your senses?

Come down from your fences, open the gate.

It may be rainin', but there's a rainbow above you.

You'd better let somebody love you before it's too late."[3] *The Eagles*

What will you choose? Each of us must decide, and God honors our choice. Stop standing in the middle ground. Step out of the rain and into His grace.

Why Are Things Still Broken?

If Jesus has already won, why does the world still look so broken? Why does evil persist? Why do we continue to struggle, and why do the headlines seem to echo defeat? Scripture offers several answers.

The current adversary still prowls.

Satan's authority was shattered at the cross, but he has not yet been removed. His rule has ended, yet he still exerts influence. Scripture describes him as a lion prowling for prey. He is a defeated foe, but one who continues to fight fierce-ly. Like a defeated army refusing to accept its loss, the powers of darkness lash out in desperation, aware that their time is running short.

Our dual nature.

Through Jesus, our spirits are reborn, yet our old nature still clings to us. We have inherited the second Adam's new, grace-filled nature, but our former instincts remain. Scripture describes this tension as an inner conflict: "I do the very thing I hate."[4] The chains of sin have been broken, yet their echoes still linger. We are free, but we often live as if we are not.

I once saw a video where the screen had been removed from a door, yet the family dog refused to step through. Even when the owner walked through the empty frame to show there was no barrier, the dog would not move. Only when the owner opened the door with the nonexistent screen did the dog finally cross over. Step across, my friend. The barrier is gone. You can know the truth, and the truth will set you free.

Those who have not chosen.

Many continue to follow in the footsteps of the old Adam, placing their confidence in themselves and walking their own path. The way of self-cen-teredness and control leads inevitably to a life consumed by lust, greed, anger, and every other force that corrodes the soul and society alike.

It is why creation still groans. Countless people remain under the Kingdom of Darkness, bound to its deception and its ruler.

A window of time to reclaim the nations.

After the Tower of Babel, the nations scattered and pledged their loyalty to other powers. Out of this dispersion, Israel became God's chosen starting point, the nation through whom the true King would come. The decisive victory has already been won, yet God's patience continues. As we will see, Jesus is gathering a new people, drawn from every tribe, language, and nation, before the end unfolds.

These are among the reasons the world remains broken. The victory is assured, but the story is still unfolding. God's work continues as He forms a new people from every nation, preparing them for their role in His kingdom.

The Mystery Revealed

From the beginning, God made promises to His people. To Abraham, He vowed that all nations would be blessed through his descendants. To David, He promised that one of his offspring would reign on the throne forever. Through the prophets, He declared that a King would come to make all things right. Again and again, Israel heard His covenant words: "I will be your God, and you will be my people."[5]

These promises were never abandoned. Israel remained God's chosen vessel, and through her, the promised King arrived, and that King was God Himself.

Yet between the King's first coming and His future return to take the throne, something astonishing occurred. Scripture calls it a mystery—a truth once hidden through the ages but now made known.

After the resurrection, when Jesus met with His followers—those who have put their trusting loyalty in Him—for the final time, He gave them their mission. They were to make disciples, beginning in Israel. Then He added something new: "All authority in heaven and on earth has been given to me."[6] With those words, He declared that the authority, lost by Adam, claimed by Satan, further divided at Babel, had now been reclaimed. The nations that had fallen under lesser spiritual powers were now His to rescue. That is why the mission did not stop in Israel but expanded to the "uttermost parts of the earth."[7]

God is forming a new community, not drawn from one nation but from every nation under heaven.

Scripture gives many names for those who belong to Jesus. Some are names He spoke Himself, such as friends and brothers. Others include saints, heirs, sons and daughters, and living stones in His temple. No single title can capture this identity, for no single word is vast enough to describe how finite people are joined to an infinite God.

Yet one name rises above them all. Scripture calls these redeemed people the Bride.

Not merely subjects of a kingdom, but partners in intimate union.

Not simply welcomed, but exalted.

Not only forgiven, but invited to reign.

To be the Bride is to be united with Christ, sharing His inheritance and ruling at His side. Our eternal calling is not just to dwell in the renewed creation, but to reign with the King from the Eternal City. It has always been God's design, a loving family to fill the earth and a Bride for the Son, a people destined to rule beside Him forever.

In the meantime . . .

Remember, God's new people are not reformed by learned behavior. They are transformed through a new, inherited nature. We live in a world filled with religions and systems of rules that tell us what to do and what not to do: follow this law, wear that style, avoid certain foods, listen only to certain music.

If we have chosen "The Way" by placing our trust in Jesus, we have that new nature. With this new life comes a two-fold assignment to grow in our new nature so we can connect with others in meaningful ways.

First, let's look at how that applies with each other: We are to love God with all our heart and love our neighbor as ourselves.[8] That is what it means to be a disciple of Jesus—learning to live in wisdom shaped by love. (As opposed to the old way of living in foolishness shaped by selfishness.) Every person and every situation is unique. As we grow, we are transformed to love others as Jesus loves, and this is more than a call to harmony. Scripture tells us that the world will recognize that we follow Jesus by the way we love one another. How we treat one another, even in disagreement, demonstrates the truth of who Jesus is. Trusting in what He has done for us gives us the power to live this way.

Second, let's see how this applies with the world—the people around us: Our relationships with each other prepare us to reach those who have not yet encountered this truth. We are called to extend the choice to others, helping them see through the confusion of the world and inviting them into the truth we've discovered—the reality of God's kingdom. We invite them to witness and experience the truth in us, and through this, to join the Bride and share in the life of the kingdom.

Jesus once told a story about a king who prepared a wedding banquet. Invitations were sent, but many who received them refused to come. Some were too busy, others made excuses, and some even mocked the messengers. The king then sent his servants out again, this time into the streets and alleys, inviting anyone they could find. Before long, the hall was filled with guests who had never expected to be there.

The point is clear: God has prepared a feast, and He invites us to join Him. Part of our responsibility is to carry that invitation. Like the servants in the story, we are sent into the world to extend the offer to others. An invitation does no good if it is ignored, but it also does no good if it is never delivered. The door is open, yet people must hear that they are welcome to walk through it.

What Comes Next?

The Kingdom has begun, but it is not yet complete. The decisive victory has already been won, yet the final chapter is still ahead.

Israel's expectations of their Messiah-King were not wrong; their timing was. The King will come again, this time to reign fully as the second Adam, ushering in the Kingdom of light.

The opportunity to choose will not remain open forever. When the King returns, the age of invitation will end. Battle lines will be drawn, the war against the Domain of Darkness will reach its conclusion, and every rival will fall. Every injustice will be addressed, and every enemy will be silenced. The King is returning, not to offer rescue this time, but to reclaim His world once and for all.

Chapter 11

The Return of the King, Part 2

A Sobering Reality

Up to this point in our story, we've looked mostly backward. We traced the beginnings in Eden, the rebellion, God's promises, the broken religions of humanity, the victory of the God-Man—the Messiah-King, and the Great Invitation that still echoes in the present. Now we turn forward. Ahead lies what Scripture calls the end of the age—events not yet seen, but certain to unfold. It is a sobering path to consider.

At some point, God will bring human history, as we know it, to a close. Events will occur that are difficult to fathom. We live in a broken world, a world in rebellion against its Creator. When Jesus returns, He will not come as a baby in a manger. He will come as King to reclaim the world that became His at the resurrection. Yet the fallen spiritual powers of darkness will not surrender quietly. It will be a war—light against darkness, truth against deception—and humanity will be caught in the struggle.

During that time, God's justice will be absolute and swift. For many readers, these descriptions may feel harsh or jarring. Part of the difficulty is that broken people in a broken world carry a distorted picture of reality. We struggle to understand what true justice looks like.

The reason is simple: we judge ourselves by comparison, not by truth. When we evaluate our lives, we rarely measure against God's holiness. Instead, we compare ourselves to the people around us. In my generation, and perhaps still today, Hitler is often regarded as the ultimate standard of evil. The unspoken assumption is that as long as there are people worse than me, I'm doing all right. We expect God to grade on a curve. Scripture tells us otherwise: He will not.

True justice unsettles us because we find it hard to imagine judgment falling on someone for actions we ourselves might commit. If they do not receive mercy, we know we wouldn't either—and that unsettles us.

The reality is this: the only reason any of us are alive and breathing today—the only reason this world has not collapsed into utter chaos—is God's mercy. From the very beginning, God warned Adam and Eve that if they ate from the tree of the knowledge of good and evil, they would surely die. And yet He delayed that sentence as an act of patience, mercy, and loving kindness.

Think of it this way. Imagine a teacher who sets a clear rule: homework is due every Friday at the start of class. For half the year, the teacher quietly allows submission until Monday. Then, after Christmas break, the original rule returns—Friday. The first week a student misses the deadline, they receive an F. The reaction is anger or outrage. Why? Because mercy had been extended so long that it felt like the rule itself. Mercy became the expectation, and justice felt unfair.

It is how many will feel when reading about the End Times. We have lived under God's grace and mercy our entire lives. But justice is coming. When it arrives, it will not be graded on a curve. God's standard is His own holiness, and His Word is clear: "The wages of sin is death."[1]

Revelation and Choice

Before moving forward, it's important to recall what we explored in Chapter 3 about God's revelation and humanity's response.

God freely offers general revelation to all people. The design and beauty of creation proclaim His presence. He has also written eternity on our hearts. Deep down, we recognize that the world does not operate as it was intended. Even though we are broken, as His image-bearers we carry a moral framework—a conscience that whispers right from wrong.

This gift carries a danger. If we continually deny and act against what God has made plain, our hearts harden. Scripture says that at some point God "gives us over"[2] to follow the desires we insist on pursuing. He did this corporately at Babel, scattering nations that rejected Him, and He does it individually when people persist in rebellion.

The opposite is also true. When we acknowledge the truth before us and align our lives with it, God promises, "If you seek me with all your heart, you will find me." He guides us through the noise and distortion—like a hidden image emerging from a stereogram—into the deeper reality of His truth.

This deeper truth comes through what God has chosen to reveal: in Scripture, and in the person of Jesus. Those who recognize this revelation and place their trust in what Jesus accomplished through His death and resurrection discover a path of light and eternal life.

For those who reject it, God still honors their choice. He gives them over to the way they insist on living. It may seem right in their own eyes, but Scripture is clear about where it leads: chaos, darkness, and ultimately eternal separation.

A Glimpse Ahead

Those reminders form our foundation as we consider what lies ahead.

We are now stepping into a brief overview of the End-Times events leading to The Return of Heaven. Entire libraries have been written on these topics—many with intricate detail that can be difficult to understand. That's not surprising. Much of what God reveals about the future isn't meant to let us chart every moment in advance, but so that those living through these times will recognize them when they arrive.

Faithful followers of Jesus may differ on certain details, and much about the future remains shrouded in mystery. What we can know with certainty is that Jesus wins, evil is defeated, and the Kingdom is established forever.

With this in mind, we'll continue exploring the story through my understanding of these events. Keep in mind what we discussed in the Ground Rules chapter.

We're about to enter uncharted waters for many readers, and it can feel like a lot to take in. Don't worry—understanding grows over time. Knowledge on this topic will, like a seed, germinate slowly. Each time you revisit it, you'll likely see it more clearly.

And like other difficult and wondrous parts of this story, these themes carry depths far beyond what a single chapter can hold. As we move forward, the focus will remain on understanding the unfolding of God's plan—not on satisfying curiosity about hidden details. That's a rabbit trail that never ends.

For Those Who Chose Loving Loyalty To The Messiah-King

At times, it may feel as though God is silent or distant. To many, it seems He has stepped back, allowing humanity to stumble under the weight of its own choices. The truth, however, is far different. God is always active in the world—often working quietly behind the scenes. Yet throughout history, there have been moments when God broke into the story in unmistakable ways: Creation, the Fall, the Flood, Babel and the scattering of the nations, the Exodus, the virgin birth, and the resurrection, to name a few.

It has been some time since God has moved in history with such dramatic force. For many, that delay has led to spiritual complacency. Yet the next move of God will astonish the world.

The Rapture

The rapture is an event yet to come, when the Messiah-King calls all His people home. He will call them up and meet them in the clouds. This echoes the ancient wedding language we explored earlier, where the Groom comes to claim His Bride and take her to her new home.

For those alive when this happens, we will be changed—transformed in an instant. Our body and soul will take on the same new nature as our spirit, which was made alive when we placed our trust in the work of our King at His resurrection.

For those who have already died, their living soul and spirit in heaven will be reunited with their new, resurrected bodies.

Scripture describes this event:

"And regarding the question, friends, about those who have already died, we do not want you in the dark. First, you must not grieve as people who have no hope, as if the grave were the last word. Since Jesus died and broke free from the grave, God will certainly bring back to life those who died in Jesus. And here is the sequence: We can tell you with complete confidence, with the Master's word, that when the Master comes again, those of us who are still alive will not go ahead of the dead and leave them behind. In fact, they will rise first. The Master himself will give the command, the archangel will sound, and God's trumpet will blow. The dead in Christ will rise—they will go first. Then the rest of us who are still alive at that time will be caught up with them into the clouds to meet the Master. We will all be together in a great family reunion with the Master. Encourage one another with these words."[3]

To the watching world, it may seem as though His followers have simply disappeared. But for those caught up, it will be a response to the shout of the King as we rise to meet Him in the air. Those who have already died in faith will have their souls and spirits reunited with their new bodies, and together we will rendezvous with the Lord in the clouds as He takes us home.

The Judgment Seat of Christ

This is an event for the faithful followers of the Messiah-King. Though the word judgment is used, it is more akin to an awards ceremony.

While events unfold on earth, those caught up to heaven will stand before the Judgment Seat of Christ. It is not a trial to determine guilt or innocence—that was settled at the cross: "Who the Son sets free is free indeed."[4] This is for reward.

The picture is not that of a courtroom but of a general returning from battle, distributing medals of honor to his troops.

Scripture speaks of rewards in heaven, most of which appear to be connected to our span of responsibility in The Return of Heaven. But here we need to put our color-blind glasses back on. I don't believe there will be emotions of loss, shame, or envy—only joy in the recognition we receive, and delight in the honors given to those we love.

We'll explore rewards further in Chapter 13, and it's a subject with beautiful depth—more than these few pages can fully unfold.

The Marriage Supper of the Lamb

From there, the scene shifts to joy beyond description—the culmination of the Great Invitation. Scripture calls it the Marriage Supper of the Lamb, the grandest celebration in the history of creation. Even the most lavish earthly galas or state ceremonies pale in comparison. This is a banquet prepared and hosted by the Creator Himself.

Can we imagine it fully? Not entirely. Scripture says, "No eye has seen, no ear has heard, no human mind has conceived the things God has prepared for those who love him."[5] But what we do know is this: in that moment, the Bride is recognized as joined to the Son, forever His. We become co-heirs of the Kingdom and will reign with Him.

Meanwhile Back on Earth

In the aftermath of the Rapture, the world will reel. Families will be suddenly broken apart, workplaces will miss key people, and governments will find leaders inexplicably gone. The disruption will be profound. Confusion will spread rapidly, and with it, fear.

We've already seen how global events can reshape daily life and how populations may accept sweeping restrictions for the promise of safety. Now imagine that dynamic magnified on a worldwide scale. This time is often referred to as *The Great Tribulation*, and out of this chaos a leader will rise.

At first, he will appear to be a savior—promising peace, order, and stability. He will rally the nations under his authority. Scripture is clear, however, that his power does not originate from his own brilliance or charisma but from Satan. This man of lawlessness, the one we call the Antichrist, will embody humanity's rebellion. He is the result of God "giving people over" to the desires they have repeatedly chosen. By this stage of the story, most of the world will have rejected God's truth and will eagerly follow a ruler who reflects their defiance.

Scripture also speaks of a Restrainer.[6] This is the third Person of the Trinity—the Holy Spirit. Through the ages, the Spirit of God has held back lawlessness and will continue to do so until the appointed time. When that restraint is lifted, the man of lawlessness will be revealed. Evil will run unchecked, and humanity will plunge headlong down the path it has chosen. This is not God forcing judgment but the natural outworking of long-standing rebellion.

Initially, the Antichrist's promises will sound convincing, especially to Israel, to whom he will offer protection. Yet his treaty will be deception. His mission is conquest and control. Under his rule, a one-world system of power will emerge. Economies will be tied to allegiance; access to resources and survival will depend on submission to his authority. Through financial systems, identification marks, or digital controls, there will be nowhere to hide. Those who resist and remain faithful to the Messiah-King will be marked as rebels, and many will seal their faith with their lives.

Meanwhile, the world will convulse. Scripture describes the judgments of this period as *"birth pains."*[7] Like labor contractions, they will come with increasing frequency and intensity. Wars, famine, and disasters will escalate until natural catastrophe seems to merge with supernatural wrath. By the time the final confrontation approaches, well over half of humanity will have perished through conflict, collapse, and catastrophe.

The story moves swiftly toward its climax. The armies of the earth will gather in northern Israel, in the Valley of Megiddo—a real location that has witnessed countless battles throughout history but none like the one to come. In Scripture, the Hebrew name is *Har Megiddo,* meaning "the hill of Megiddo." Over centuries, the name traveled through Greek, Latin, and English, becoming *Armageddon*—a word loaded with finality.

Popular culture often turns Armageddon into a symbol of catastrophe or humanity uniting against evil. Scripture tells a different story. The nations are not uniting to save the world; they are uniting to defy God. This is not good trying to stop evil—it is evil trying to stop good.

And just when darkness reaches its height, the sky will open.

The King will return.

History's darkest hour becomes the stage for its brightest dawn. Just as the false leader, the Antichrist, begins to march toward Jerusalem, Heaven breaks into the earthly dimension. The world sees the King. The Antichrist repositions his armies to confront Him.

I could describe the King's return, but perhaps it is better to read it together:

"And I saw heaven opened, and behold, a white horse, and He who sat on it is called Faithful and true, and in righteousness He judges and wages war. His eyes are a flame of fire, and on His head are many crowns; and He has a name written on Him which no one knows except Himself. He is clothed with a robe dipped in blood, and His name is called The Word of God. And the armies which are in heaven, clothed in fine linen, white and clean, were following Him on white horses. From His mouth comes a sharp sword, so that with it He may strike down the nations, and He will rule them with a rod of iron; and He treads the wine press of the fierce wrath of God, the Almighty. And on His robe and on His thigh He has a name written: 'KING OF KINGS, AND LORD OF LORDS.'

And I saw the beast [the Antichrist] and the kings of the earth and their armies, assembled to make war against Him who sat on the horse, and against His army."

"And the beast was seized, along with the false prophet who performed the signs in his presence, deceiving those who had received the mark of the beast and those who worshiped his image. These two were thrown alive into the lake of fire, which burns with brimstone. The rest were killed with the sword that came from the mouth of Him who sat on the horse, and all the birds were filled with their flesh."[8]

The return of the King is almost anticlimactic. His justice is swift and absolute. The same God who said, "Let there be light,"[9] now speaks, not to create life, but to bring death to the armies of darkness.

The battle concludes with the King and His army separating the survivors—the faithful and those who defied Him to the end. The defiers meet death and are ushered into Sheol, the waiting place of the dead. Satan is captured, bound, and sealed away for a final act and coming judgment. The surviving faithful will reign with the King for 1,000 years, along with the martyrs who are raised to life. This is not yet The Return of Heaven, the Eternal City. This period is called the Millennial Kingdom.

The Millennial Kingdom

With the battle ended and evil restrained, creation enters a new age—the Millennial Kingdom.

During these years, the earth will be populated by the offspring of the faithful survivors of the Great Tribulation. These descendants remain part of fallen humanity, still faced with the same choices each of us confronts.

The Millennial reign is described as a peaceful kingdom—free from war, ruled in partnership by God and restored humanity, and filled with the true knowledge of God. Parts of the Adamic curse will be removed: "The wolf will dwell with the lamb,"[10] physical ailments will cease, and sorrow and crying will be no more. It is a world of perfect justice.

As the thousand years conclude, an unexpected event occurs. Humanity will have repopulated the planet—thriving in peace, health, and prosperity, with numbers like the sand of the seashore. Satan is released from his prison and once again deceives the nations. They gather to wage war on Jerusalem, but no battle is fought. Fire comes down from heaven and devours them. It is over. Satan is thrown into the Lake of Fire, joining the Antichrist and the false prophet, never to rise again.

Promises Made. Promises Kept.

The Millennial Kingdom is not a random interlude in God's plan; it is the visible proof that every promise He made will be fulfilled.

To Abraham, God pledged a land and descendants that would bless the nations.[11]

To David, He promised a throne that would never end.[12]

Through the prophets, He spoke of Israel's restoration, justice flowing like rivers, and peace covering the earth.[13]

For generations, skeptics have dismissed these promises as symbolic or unfulfilled. The Millennium leaves no doubt: God's Word stands. What He declares, He accomplishes. His covenants are not vague spiritual ideas but solid realities that history itself will testify to. God fulfilled them not through a clean "do-over" free from hardship or opposition, but within a broken, rebellious, and cursed world.

Humanity Left Without Excuse

The Millennium also exposes the true depth of humanity's problem. For a thousand years, people will live in conditions unlike anything since Eden—peace, abundance, justice, and the righteous reign of the Messiah-King. Yet when Satan is released at the end, multitudes will rush to follow him. Why? Because rebellion runs deeper than circumstances. Sin is not simply the product of bad systems, poor parenting, or corrupt leadership. It is lodged in the human heart.

Even in a perfect world under perfect rule, fallen humanity still chooses defiance. The Millennium delivers a final verdict: humanity apart from God will always turn away. When judgment comes, no one will be able to claim innocence or say they never had the chance.

At the final judgment, the Great White Throne, everyone will be without excuse.[14]

Chapter 12

The End of the Old World Order

Faith Through The Ages

We are entering the final hour of the cursed Old World Order. Soon, all things will be made new. But God, being true to His nature as a just Judge, will not simply sweep the remnants under the rug as He finishes His work. Long ago, He told the fallen sons of God that—immortal and powerful as they seemed—they would "die like men."[1] Their judgment day has come. Scripture says the lake of fire was prepared for Satan and his fallen angels, yet for much of humanity, this will be their fate as well. It is the end for all who chose to go their own way, who did not want to be with God.

Through the ages, we have learned that removing guilt and reconnecting with God has never been about following the rules of failed, man-made religions. It has always been the consequence of a loving choice—the choice of trusting loyalty. It is choosing to believe in the words and promises of God rather than yielding to the temptations around us and the desires within us.

Theologians—those who labor to study the knowledge of God—have sought to break down this mystery to help us understand, as best as possible, the incomprehensible works of an all-powerful, all-wise, all-loving Creator. In simplified terms, salvation can be described in three prongs—three ways of understanding what it means to be right with God.

First: The Agent of Salvation

Salvation has always been about trusting loyalty—faith. Faith in who God is, in what He has promised, and in His unshakable goodness. It is precisely where Adam and Eve failed in Eden.

Second: The Object of Salvation

God's goodness is expressed in specific promises and actions at different times in history. Faith has always looked to those promises. Some examples:

- **Noah** believed God's warning of judgment and built the ark.

- **Abraham** believed in God's promise of descendants and a land of inheritance.

- **Sarah** believed God's promise of a child, though her womb was barren.

- **Rahab**, a foreigner, believed God would give Jericho into Israel's hands and acted on that trust.

- **Naaman,** a foreigner, believed God's promise of cleansing through the prophet Elisha and obeyed.

- **In the present age**, the object of salvation is the work of Jesus Himself—His life, death, and resurrection.

- **In the time of great tribulation yet to come**, a remnant will put their trust in God's victory through the Messiah-King, even at the cost of their lives.

These stories remind us that while the object of faith varied through time, the agent was always the same: trusting loyalty—faith.

Third: The Basis of Salvation

Trusting loyalty has always been the means, and God's promise has always been the focus. The basis of salvation, however, has never changed. It is always the sacrifice of the Messiah, the God-Man, Jesus.

Follow me here. Before the resurrection, the faithful did not yet enter God's presence when they died. They went to Sheol, the place of the dead. As we saw in Chapter 2, Sheol had a place of comfort for the faithful and a place of torment for the unfaithful. The faithful were counted righteous before God, yet the debt of sin remained unpaid—their spirits were still dead and their nature incompatible with His. When Jesus died and rose again, that debt was erased. When He returned to the Father, He emptied the place of comfort, bringing the faithful with Him into God's presence at last.

Salvation has always been about trusting loyalty in the goodness of God. In our age, that goodness is displayed most clearly in the Messiah-King's victory. Jesus paid our debt, broke the chains of our slavery, and conquered death itself. Across all time, the basis of being right with God is the same: the wrath-ending sacrifice and triumphant resurrection of the Messiah-King.

Courtroom Scene

Having seen how salvation has always worked through faith in God's goodness, we now come to the final reckoning: the courtroom of the Great White Throne.

Before the trial begins, we are introduced to the officers of this court. Jesus, the Messiah-King, presides as Judge with the final say. Scripture also tells us that the Bride has a role: "Or do you not know that the Lord's people will judge the world? ... Do you not know that we will judge angels?"[2] Exactly how that looks remains mysterious. Perhaps the Bride will serve as a jury alongside the Judge, or perhaps in another role within His divine council. What is clear is that in sharing His reign, the Bride also shares His judgments. Angels too fill the courtroom as witnesses. It is not chaos, but order. The terror of the moment does not erase the structure of justice. It fulfills it.

Let us look together:

"Then I saw a great white throne and Him who sat upon it, from whose presence earth and heaven fled, and no place was found for them."[3]

Can you feel the sense of dread in this scene? Have you ever felt dread yourself? I have, a few times. It's unbearable. Fear and dread are not the same. Fear triggers adrenaline and the fight-or-flight response. Dread is worse. It seeps into your soul, creating despair, hopelessness, a sense of becoming undone. It is like a heavy shadow falling over you, making you feel powerless, exposed, and ready to crumble.

That is what this moment will be like as fallen spiritual and physical beings stand before an unshrouded, holy God in all His glory. When one finally sees God for who He truly is, one also sees oneself for who they truly are—how deep the treachery runs, how dark the rebellion has been. That is dread.

To grasp this, imagine standing there. You are enclosed in glass—no escape, nowhere to hide. The Judge sits on the throne. Around Him stands the Bride, with regal authority, and multitudes of faithful followers. Angels fill the court as witnesses. Suddenly, you are stripped bare. A record of your life begins to play—a movie of every action, every word, every hidden thought. Nothing is left unexposed. This is dread.

Let us continue reading:

"And I saw the dead, the great and the small, standing before the throne ..."[4]

No one is exempt. In our world, we know the sting of a two-tiered justice system. The wealthy, the powerful, and the well-connected often escape accountability, while the weak and poor bear the full weight of the law. It feels unfair. But not here. Before this throne, there is no privilege, no political leverage, no behind-the-scenes influence. Kings and commoners, generals and foot soldiers, rulers and peasants alike will stand before the Judge of all the earth. Here, at last, perfect justice is done.

Trial proceedings

The trial proceedings now begin. Let us look together:

"And the books were opened; and another book was opened, which is the book of life; and the dead were judged from the things which were written in the books, according

to their deeds. And the sea gave up the dead who were in it, and Death and Hades gave up the dead who were in them; and they were judged, each one of them according to their deeds."⁵

We see two kinds of records here: "the books" and "another book." That other book is the *Book of Life*. The first phase of this trial is swift and simple: Is your name written in the Book of Life?

How does one's name come to be recorded there? Very simply: by being among those trusting, loyal followers we have discussed throughout this book—those who have received their freedom through the debt paid on their behalf by the King. For this group appearing at this judgment, tragically, none will have their names written.

"Is their name in the Book of Life?"

"No, my King."

"Guilty."

Swift, fair, immediate justice.

But the passage also speaks of the "the books," where the dead are judged according to their deeds. This is the punishment phase of the trial. The severity of punishment aligns perfectly with one's choices. God is love, yet love is not love without choice. Choice is not choice without consequences. A just God ensures that consequences fit the choices exactly.

At this moment, one might think, *At least I am not Hitler.* And it is true—those who rejected God and committed unspeakable evil will face severe judgment. But consider also the one who never committed atrocities, who was raised by godly parents, who heard the truth of Jesus' death and resurrection, and whose friends modeled His loving wisdom—yet still chose their own way. Their accountability is greater because of what they knew and rejected. Their punishment is just as certain.

Dread.

Eternal Separation

As we begin to conclude this part of our journey, we are confronted with the sobering reality that for these people, this will be their state of existence for all eternity. Beyond the legal concepts of guilt and punishment, there is a deeper truth: this is the natural state of being separated from the Creator.

Even the faithful followers of old had to wait until the resurrection to enter God's presence. It was not due to a lack of faith but because their nature was incompatible with God's. Until the Messiah's sacrifice, their debt had not been paid, preventing their spirits from being fully reborn and reunited with the Source of Life.

Any person who chooses not to accept the pardon offered by the Messiah-King is choosing to remain disconnected from the Source of Life. Their very nature continues to be incompatible with His. Imagine an ice cube placed in a furnace—it would instantly melt. In the same way, separation from God is not merely a legal problem; it is a problem of fundamental incompatibility. It simply . . . is.

Scripture teaches that while we all had a beginning, we have no end. Our essence exists forever. It also teaches that Jesus, the Messiah-King, is the Creator and Sustainer of all things and that in Him all things hold together.[6] What then, is the natural state of a being created to exist forever when separated from the One who holds all things together?

One description I have heard likens it to being trapped within a private nuclear explosion—an eruption of energy that can never fully release, never find completion. It is a kind of eternal unraveling.

In the end, those who have chosen life apart from God, disconnected from the Source of Life, find themselves doubly unprepared. They are not equipped to exist in His holy presence, yet neither are they equipped to meaningfully exist apart from His sustaining presence.

It is the dread of eternal separation.

The judgment of the Great White Throne does not mark the end of the story; it marks the end of an old story. The curse, the rebellion, and all who chose to go their own way are brought to justice. The Old World Order is finished.

What comes next is entirely new. The next chapter opens not with darkness, but with dawn. Not with separation, but with reunion. Not with despair, but with hope fulfilled.

Chapter 13

The Return Of Heaven

"This certainly is not the best of all possible worlds; but it may very well be the only way to the best of all possible worlds."[1]

— Dr. Al McCallister, PhD, Columbia International University, c. 1988–89

Introduction

This book has taken us on a journey. Our lives have been journeys, too. And the world itself has traveled a long, winding road, marked with both beauty and heartbreak. Few would call it the best of all possible worlds. Yet somehow, this seems to be the way God has chosen to lead us toward the best world to come.

Consider this: our greatest strengths rarely emerge in comfort. They are forged in fire. The colors of a ceramic vessel appear only through the heat of the kiln. The joy of holding a newborn child comes only after the labor pains that precede it. The resurrection followed the suffering of the cross. Compassion is learned not in theory, but in the ache of loss and the weight of tears. Even nature whispers this pattern: a seed must fall into the ground and die before it can bring forth new life.

So it has been throughout human history—progress through pain, growth through struggle, hope shining brightest against the backdrop of despair.

In the previous chapter, we witnessed death itself and the place of the dead cast into the lake of fire, never to rise again. The past is gone. The Old World Order has collapsed. Pain and loss, regret and guilt, loneliness and fear, striving and anxiety—all gone.

Now, at last, all things are made new. The reality will surpass anything we can imagine.

Welcome to The Return of Heaven.

CHAPTER 13—Book One: The Place of Heaven

New Heaven and New Earth

In first-century Jewish culture, when a man sought to marry a woman, he first spoke with her father. The father gave his daughter away, and the groom-to-be paid a price—not to purchase her, but to demonstrate her worth and to show that he could care for her. Once the couple agreed, they entered a betrothal. Though not yet consummated, the agreement was legally binding.

The groom then returned to his father's house and began building a home for himself and his bride. Only when the dwelling was complete would he return, take her in procession, and bring her into their new home after a joyful wedding feast.

In much the same way, Jesus prayed to the Father, thanking Him for "those you have given me."[2] He also paid the ultimate price for His bride—His own life. By placing our loyal trust in Him, our Messiah-King who reclaimed the kingdom, we are betrothed to Him. We are not yet married, but already His.

At the Last Supper, just before His arrest, Jesus prepared His followers for what was to come. He comforted them with these words:

"Do not let your hearts be troubled. Believe in God; believe also in me. In My Father's house are many rooms. If it were not so, would I have told you that I go to prepare a place for you? And if I go and prepare a place for you, I will come again and take you to myself, that where I am, you may be also."[3]

This is wedding language. He is preparing a place for us so that He may come and take us to Himself. We have already seen this begin to play out in the rapture, followed by His wedding banquet. From that moment forward, the Bride is with her Bridegroom forever, reigning alongside Him as His queen.

From there, the story carries us through the Millennial Kingdom and the Great Judgment until, at last, John's vision opens:

"[The angel] spoke to me, saying, 'Come, I will show you the Bride, the wife of the Lamb.' And he carried me away in the Spirit to a great, high mountain, and showed me the holy city, Jerusalem, coming down out of heaven from God."[4]

The Eternal City—the New Jerusalem, the City of Peace—the new Eden and the dwelling place of God. It is our home, the place He has prepared for us. Here, at last, Heaven itself returns, God dwelling with His people, face to face. This is The Return of Heaven.

The Eternal City

Out of more than 750,000 words in the Bible, only about 2,500—less than half of one percent—describe the eternal state. God gives glimpses, not blueprints. A bird's-eye view, not floor plans. Perhaps that is because we could not begin to comprehend the realities of that world. Does time operate the same way? Does space? We do not know. What we do know is breathtaking.

The Scale of the City

The city is enormous—1,500 miles wide, long, and tall. A perfect cube. Its walls shimmer like translucent jasper, set with every kind of precious stone. At its center, God dwells, His glory blazing through it all.

Some imagine the city suspended above the new earth, its radiance lighting the world below. Picture looking up, not to see the sun we know, but a diamond-like city refracting every color across the sky. The Father's glory shines like the sun itself, and Scripture says the Lamb—the Messiah-King—is its Lamp. Perhaps His glory streams outward like ribbons of aurora, illuminating even the night side of the planet. What a sight it will be.

The Structure of the City

John describes the city as having no night. Its brilliance never fades. Yet on the newly created earth, nations "walk by its light,"[5] suggesting that the earth itself may still have a rhythm of day and night, but is fully illuminated by God's glory.

The city has three gates on each of its four sides—twelve in all—each made of a single, giant pearl. Its walls rise high, and the streets are pure gold, refined like transparent glass. John describes the street of the city—singular. Perhaps one vast main street runs through the city's heart, leading to the throne where God Himself dwells.

Like Eden, the city has a river—the River of Life—flowing clear from the throne. There is also the Tree of Life, planted on either side of the river. How can one tree span both sides? We are not told. Perhaps its trunk is unimaginably vast, the river flowing through its base. Or perhaps the vision is meant to stretch our imagination.

The Family of God in the Age to Come

The Eternal City is alive with people and beings. At its center is the Triune God Himself: the Father, the Son—our King Jesus—and the Holy Spirit. All life, love, and glory flow from Him.

Next is the Bride of Christ, those who placed their trust in the death and resurrection of the Messiah-King. They are indwelt with His Spirit, made partakers of the divine nature, raised with resurrected bodies like His, and called to reign at His side.

Then come the Faithful through the Ages, the citizens of the new earth. This group includes:

The spirits of the righteous made perfect, those who trusted God from the beginning of time until the resurrection.

The Millennial Kingdom survivors, followers who remained faithful for the thousand years and entered the New Heaven and New Earth.

The Tribulation Martyrs are also given a distinct honor. Scripture places them before the throne of God, serving Him in His presence. They are part of the eternal household, though in a role different from the Bride or the nations.

Finally, the Spiritual Beings—cherubim, seraphim, archangels, messengers, warriors, and perhaps others not yet revealed—dwell in God's household, each with dignity, purpose, and joy.

God's family is vast and varied, yet perfectly united. From the throne, His love binds the Bride, the citizens of earth, the martyrs, and the heavenly host into one eternal household.

The Home of the Bride

For all who belong to Him, the Eternal City is not just a destination to visit; it is home. Jesus said, "In My Father's house are many rooms... I go to prepare a place for you." The Eternal City is that house—the place He has prepared for His Bride.

In the ancient world, a groom would return to his father's estate and build an addition, a room, for his bride. In the same way, Jesus prepares a dwelling for each of us within His Father's house—the Eternal City itself.

And what might those dwellings be like? Ancient cities often had people living within their massive walls. Could the same be true here? Imagine the walls of this city—stretching 1,500 miles high—holding dwelling places for the Bride. From one window, you might gaze out across the majestic, newly created earth; from another, look inward toward the radiant heart of the city, beholding the glory of God's throne.

We can only speculate about the details. Whatever picture we sketch will fall short of reality. But this much we know: the Eternal City is the Father's house, the home of the Bride, and the dwelling place of God with His people forever. It will be more beautiful, more alive, and more filled with love than we can yet imagine.

The New Earth

Scripture tells us far more about the Eternal City than it does about the new earth itself. But one unique detail stands out: "there will be no seas."[6]

That short phrase is quietly explosive. A world without oceans is not this one drained of water—it signals an entirely new order of creation. Today, the seas govern weather, regulate climate, sustain ecosystems, and hold most of Earth's life. Remove them, and everything changes. It won't be a repaired world—it will be a new one. The old has passed away, and what rises in its place will be unfamiliar, wondrous, and beyond imagination.

The absence of oceans also raises the question of food. Will we even need food in the world to come? If so, it will not be at the expense of another life, for death will be no more. Yet Scripture depicts scenes of feasting and dining. I sense that, for some, food may not be required to sustain the body, but for all, meals will remain moments of joy, celebration, connection, and community.

Consider the scale: if the new earth is the same size as the current one, yet no longer seventy percent covered by water, imagine the space that remains. Perhaps it reflects the vastness of God's gathered family.

So when you feel small and solitary in your faith—as if you are one of only a few who truly trust God—remember this truth. One of the enemy's favorite lies is that we are alone. One day, however, the multitude of God's people will be so great that an entire new planet will be needed to hold them all. We are not alone. Our faith is not in vain.

Think of the beauty of our world today—the snowcapped mountains, a peaceful lakeside reflecting autumn leaves, the roar of a waterfall, the vast expanse of a star-filled sky, the colors of a sunset, the delicate petals of a flower. Even under the weight of the curse, these things take our breath away. Now imagine the new, perfect world—designed to reflect God's beauty and adorned to honor His presence.

The New Earth is the canvas, but the story does not end with its scale or beauty. The true wonder lies in how it will be filled—with nations walking in God's light, with kings bringing their glory into the City, and with God's people discovering what life in eternity was always meant to be.

CHAPTER 13—Book Two: The Life of Heaven

Zoe Life

When we examine the New Testament in its original Greek, we find three distinct words translated into the single English word life.

Bios (bee-os) refers to physical life, our biological existence, the temporary life of the body.

Psuche (soo-khay) refers to soul-life, the seat of our mind, emotions, and will.

Zoe (dzo-ay) refers to divine, spiritual life; life that comes from God and is sustained by God.

When Scripture speaks of eternal life, it is not merely describing life that never ends. It is describing Zoe life—a life that flows directly from the Source of all life. Yes, it is everlasting, but more than that, it is an unbroken connection to God Himself.

The natural (fallen) person, Scripture says, is spiritually dead—cut off from the Source of life and enslaved to broken desires and the dark powers that dominate the world. The transformed person now carries two natures: the renewed spirit longs for God, but the old nature still resists. The struggle is constant. In the world to come, that struggle ends. Every part of our being—body, soul, and spirit—will be made new, complete, whole, and glorious. Zoe Life.

Zoe Life is unbroken life—overflowing, abundant, and joyful. It never fades, never strives, never decays. It rejoices continually in the glory of its Source. Like rivers of living water, it flows from God Himself, filling every aspect of our existence.

This Zoe Life is also life at rest.

Rest Restored

To understand rest, we must first look back to the curse that followed humanity's rebellion.

Adam found himself in a state of striving. The very ground resisted him. For humanity, the world pushed back—thorns, weeds, tangled cords, broken tools, floods, and droughts. Everything required effort. Humans could never let their guard down—never truly rest.

Eve's striving was different. Her struggle took place in relationships. She longed for trust, harmony, and oneness, yet carried a deep fear of being used, hurt, or abandoned. That fear drove her to control, which in turn robbed her of the peace and connection she desired. While Adam battled a world that resisted him, Eve wrestled with an inner war—searching for intimacy and connection while trying to protect herself. Her mind was always in motion, striving to achieve what cannot be had in a broken world. She, too, could never rest.

But in Zoe Life, rest finally returns.

In the world to come, perfection does not mean merely moral flawlessness—it means completeness, wholeness, perfect peace. We will live active, meaningful, creative lives, but without the tension of striving. Challenges may still exist—after all, we bear the image of a creative, purposeful God—but we will approach them from a place of calm strength, not anxious toil.

Perhaps a faint glimpse of this can be imagined in a Jedi standing still amid the chaos of battle: poised, clear-minded, at peace despite the motion around them. Even this falls short, but it hints at the serenity of life in perfect harmony with our Creator.

That is Rest.

That is Zoe Life.

The Kings Bring Their Glory

In this new world, rest does not mean idleness—it is the foundation for purpose. Here, work and creativity flow not from striving, but from perfect peace.

Recall the first Eden: humanity was given a mandate to work—to rule, subdue, cultivate, and protect. That work was likely challenging, but it was not toil. It was not a fight for survival. There was no curse. It was a world of discovery, exploration, and innovation—a garden alive with potential, waiting to be developed and delighted in.

Where do we get that picture? From the second Eden—from the world to come. John writes:

"The kings of the earth will bring their glory into [the City]... and they will bring the glory and the honor of the nations into it."[7]

Notice that both kings and nations are plural. The new earth, filled with the faithful of the ages, will still have nations—distinct cultures and peoples. But this time, diversity will not divide us. Each culture will express the image of God in its own unique way, and all will move together in perfect harmony.

We are not told the details, but I imagine a society that is vibrant and creative—perhaps even high-tech beyond our comprehension—filled with people free to invent, explore, and create without corruption or decay. Great artists, musicians, choreographers, scientists, designers, engineers, architects, and roles we cannot yet conceive will all pour out their gifts with joy.

Then, together with their leaders, they will bring the best of their work into the Eternal City, to be displayed before the Messiah-King. It will be a celebration of creation, a festival of excellence, with honor and beauty flowing upward in worship to the One who gave us life and the desire to create.

Consider your own dreams, gifts, and passions. Imagine being equipped with boundless resources, wisdom, and skill—able to accomplish them with flawless joy and mastery. Imagine creating not from exhaustion or competition, but from delight. Imagine being celebrated not just by others, but by nations and by the Messiah-King Himself for the beauty and glory you have contributed to His kingdom.

How magnificent it will be to arrive on that day, only to discover that even our wildest dreams were mere shadows of the reality to come.

Reigning in the Eternal State

For example's sake, we have imagined ourselves as citizens of the new creation—the people and nations who bring their glory into the city. Yet in truth, our roles will play out differently. We are called to reign with the Messiah-King. We are not merely inhabitants of this new reality but partners in its purpose. Our calling is higher, and our joy deeper, than we can now comprehend. The One who once served us will now invite us to serve with Him—to share in His reign and reflect His glory throughout all creation.

The eternal order still includes leadership and structure: the Messiah-King reigning in glory, His Bride reigning with Him, and the kings of the earth bringing their glory into the city. Leadership in this perfect world, however, is unlike anything we have known. There is no need for laws, correction, or control, because there is no rebellion, no pride, and no sin. Every role flows in harmony with God's heart. The kingdom is ordered, not ruled; purposeful, not managed. Every act of leadership is an act of worship, reflecting the wisdom and creativity of the One who reigns forever.

In God's kingdom, leadership has always meant service. The Messiah-King redefined greatness when He knelt to wash His disciples' feet and said, "Whoever wants to be great among you must be your servant." In the eternal world, that pattern is fully realized. Those who lead will do so by nurturing others, guiding creative efforts, and equipping those they serve—much like master artists, teachers, or mentors helping others bring out the beauty God placed within them.

Perhaps much of our reigning will be expressed through serving those on the new earth, helping them discover and develop their God-given gifts, dreams, and passions for innovation and creativity.

For the Bride of the Messiah-King, reigning with Him is the fulfillment of our earthly calling. Scripture hints that faithfulness in this life—the love we have shown, the service we have offered, the perseverance we have carried—will shape the roles we are entrusted with in eternity. Crowns are not trophies of achievement but symbols of trust. What we have learned about humility, compassion, and faith will now translate into the joyful stewardship of God's restored creation.

In this perfect kingdom, among the Bride, every act of leadership and every act of service is the same. No one competes for position. Each person fully reflects the glory of God in a way that only they can. And just as each star shines with its own distinct color and brilliance—each radiating light according to its unique frequency—so too will every glorified life reflect God's glory in a way that is entirely its own.

CHAPTER 13—Book Three: The Heart of Heaven

Relationships in the Eternal State

This next topic takes some time to grasp. Today, all of our relationships are defined by roles—spouse, parent, child, friend, BFF, mentor, coworker. In the Eternal State, those distinctions will no longer exist. We will still share the treasured memories and experiences of life, but the framework of roles will be gone.

I will still know my wife as the one who was my wife, and we will cherish every memory we shared, but she will no longer be my wife. Roles will no longer define us. No doubt, that takes some processing. We must remember that trying to describe these changes is like trying to explain color to someone who is color-blind. Our closest relationships in this life, as precious as they are, will still pale in comparison to how we will perfectly know and love one another in the world to come.

And what about the physical relationship we share with our spouse? In the eternal state, we will have bodies, but not physical bodies like the ones we have now—they will be spiritual bodies. The intimacy we will experience with one another, and with God Himself, will surpass even the most beautiful expressions of physical intimacy. The love we know now is real, but it remains shadowed by the curse. Our difficulty in grasping this often comes from clinging to the shell instead of anticipating the fullness it points toward.

What about our children and our parents? Memories will remain, but the roles will no longer define us. In eternity, we share the same identity—the Bride of the Messiah-King. Children who died before adulthood will exist in what we would understand as an adult state. I lost a grandson at thirteen, and I look forward to seeing the man he is in Heaven. Similarly, those who died in old age will be renewed in youth.

What about those who died before they could understand trusting loyalty in Jesus? Those lost through miscarriage, or taken by abortion? Those with severe mental disabilities? Scripture does not speak directly to these questions, yet nearly all conservative theologians appeal to God's character—His justice, mercy, and love. They conclude that a just and merciful God would receive those who never had the capacity to understand or choose. We will see them all again, and they will be made whole.

Perfect Knowing and Perfect Loving

In this life, even the best of our relationships are filtered through limitation. We love deeply but imperfectly. We see glimpses of one another's hearts, but never the whole picture. Even our most sincere attempts at understanding fall short because we are still looking through what Scripture calls "a mirror dimly." In the world to come, that fog will lift. The veil will be gone.

Scripture says, *"Now I know in part, but then I will know fully, just as I also have been fully known."*[8] Imagine that—complete knowing and being known without hesitation or insecurity, complete love without fear of rejection. Every barrier between heart and heart, and between humanity and God, will finally disappear.

John, one of Jesus' disciples, echoed the same promise: *"We will be like Him, for we will see Him as He is."*[9] That moment will not only transform our vision of God; it will also transform how we see each other. To see Him clearly is to see truth clearly—no distortion, no hidden motives, no broken communication. Perfect love and perfect knowledge will finally coexist in perfect harmony.

Even now, the Spirit gives us glimpses of that reality. Paul, a leader among earlier followers prayed that our love would *"abound more and more in real knowledge and all discernment,"* so that we could *"approve what is excellent."*[10] In the eternal state, that prayer will be fully answered. Love will no longer need to grow—it will have arrived at its destination.

We will understand one another not through words, but through truth itself. We will not simply remember; we will comprehend. We will not merely feel affection; we will embody it. Every misunderstanding, every conflict, every wall that once stood between hearts will be gone. What remains is love that is pure, complete, and everlasting—love that reflects the very nature of God, for God is love.

When Adam and Eve fell, their first awareness was that something between them had changed. Trust gave way to fear. Openness turned to hiding. Love became guarded, filtered through shame and self-protection. Ever since, every relationship has carried the echo of that fracture—moments of misunderstanding, distance, insecurity, or loss. In the world to come, all of that will be undone. What was shattered in Eden will not only be restored; it will be made whole and overflowing. No more hiding. No more fear. Every look, every word, every embrace will carry perfect honesty and joy. The intimacy humanity once lost will be returned in greater measure than before—redeemed, purified, and sealed forever in love.

We will finally experience relationships as God intended them from the beginning: complete, unbroken, and ever-deepening. The ache that began at the eviction from Eden will end here, in the arms of perfect love.

Worship in the Eternal State

In the new world, worship will no longer be just something we do; it will be the very atmosphere we live in. God Himself dwells permanently among humanity, the intersection of Heaven and Earth made real.

Let that sink in. God Himself dwells among mankind.

What does that mean—the Creator of all things, living with us?

For some, the thought inspires pure anticipation. For others, it may feel complicated, even uncomfortable. Many picture God as they remember their fathers—loved and respected, but not someone they want watching every move. Some imagine God like electricity—vital, powerful, distant, and potentially dangerous if approached too closely. And some carry deeper wounds—fathers who ignored, hurt, or abandoned them—leaving pain and mistrust that shades how they see God.

We bring all of this baggage into how we view our heavenly Father. No wonder some want nothing to do with Him. Others love Him but quietly wish Heaven could be a parent-free vacation—a gift from God without God Himself visiting too often. Even among the faithful, that tension remains; we love Him, yet we hide from Him. But blessed are those who have learned that hiding is impossible and unnecessary. He sees everything we do and still loves us completely.

Blessed are those who have learned to wait on God, to trust His timing and goodness, to discover that His desire is not to rule over us but to dwell with us. He really, truly loves us. I imagine His presence as liquid love—something we will not merely sense or feel but experience with every part of our being. We will taste it, breathe it, move in it. Every sense—perhaps even new ones we have yet to know—will be immersed in His love.

My prayer for every reader is that you begin to break free from the hurts, fears, and betrayals of this world and start to see God for who He truly is. May you catch a glimpse, even now, of the love He has for you.

My family's genetics missed the class the day musical talent was handed out. I love music deeply; it speaks to the depth of my soul. I make attempts at the guitar and dabble a little on the drums, but I am more of a technician than a musician. Fortunately, one of my sons-in-law is a wonderful musician. I cannot think of an instrument he does not play. Some of my grandchildren now play as well. I suspect that for some, music will remain part of their growth and development, and for others, they will possess the gift and continue playing throughout their lives.

One year, several months before Christmas, my son-in-law selected music and wrote parts for each of the instruments the grandchildren played. He met with them over the phone and through video calls to help prepare for their performance. When the kids all traveled that year, we had a special treat on Christmas morning: our grandchildren presented a mini-concert for us. Keyboard, violin, flute, percussion, ukulele, and several read parts between songs came together in a wonderful telling of the Christmas story. My wife and I were deeply touched, honored, and blessed.

I think this is a glimpse of what worship is and how it blesses both us and God.

We are only beginning to scratch the surface of how sound and life interact. Early research suggests that music and natural vibration may influence the living world in ways we barely understand. Some scientists have observed that gentle sound waves can cause plants to open their stomata or alter their growth rates. Others have noticed that certain frequencies seem to boost a plant's natural defenses or stimulate blooming. A few studies even suggest that the dawn chorus of birds helps "wake up" trees and flowers—a forest-wide good-morning song that stirs creation into motion.

No one claims to have it all figured out, but discoveries like these make me wonder: what if creation really does respond to sound—not just hearing it, but feeling it—and those vibrations echo the order and beauty built into everything God made? Perhaps worship and life are woven together more deeply than we realize.

In the new creation, that harmony may no longer be subtle. Imagine our worship resonating through the new earth, stirring color, light, and life wherever it flows. The trees might shimmer brighter, the rivers sparkle more intensely, the flowers lift their faces toward the melody. Perhaps every note, heartbeat, and act of joy will ripple through creation like a wave of light—the song of Zoe Life itself. As we sing, the One who spoke the universe into being will smile as His children join the eternal song.

I imagine worship will also be times of celebration—celebrations of God's wondrous deeds. Perhaps we will have incredible technology to view His great wonders through history, or maybe we will witness them unfold in a hidden dimension beyond our current perception. Scripture does not speak of these things, but God's plans for us exceed imagination, and I offer such speculation to stretch your mind, knowing the reality will surpass anything we can conceive.

Most of us carry an outdated picture of worship. We imagine wooden pews, worn hymnals, and songs that feel centuries removed from our lives. Others picture raised hands and emotional displays that leave them wondering if it is genuine or just for show. But worship is neither dull nor performative—it is a response.

Imagine it this way: You're there for the winning goal that takes the championship. Or you're watching a walk-off home run clinch the World Series. Maybe you're in the front row at a concert by your favorite artist and they play your song—singing as if it's meant for you alone.

Think also of moments when the impossible suddenly breaks in your favor. The test results come back clean. The wayward child finally calls. The long-closed door swings open.

Imagine the roar, the tears, the unstoppable eruption of joy. Whether it comes with shouting or with silence, your whole being responds. And afterward, you replay the moment over and over in your mind.

Now multiply that moment by eternity.

That is worship—celebrating God's goodness, His wisdom, His power, and His faithful promises.

When we enter the Eternal City and stand before the throne, we will stand in awe of the Creator who made us, the Father who never gave up on us, the Son who died for us—the King who conquered death, and the Spirit who fills us and makes us partakers of the divine. The Alpha and the Omega, Who planned it all before time began, invites us into His family. How could we not worship?

Welcome Home

We have come full circle.

We have acknowledged the chaos we live in, while knowing in our hearts that it was not always this way and that it is not meant to be this way.

We have glimpsed the world that once was and reviewed the rebellious events that threw it into chaos. We have seen the futility of broken religions that teach us how to behave when what we truly need is a new nature. We have witnessed the rescue mission of our Messiah, who came to free us from the domain of darkness and restore humanity. We have been introduced to the Great Invitation and offered a choice—the sacrifice of the new Adam or the selfish, treasonous ways of the old.

We have watched as the Messiah-King returns to utterly defeat the powers of darkness and begin closing the curtain on the old world in preparation for the new creation. We have finished our journey by glimpsing the new earth and the Eternal City—the City of Peace. We have seen what Scripture reveals and imagined what may yet be, anticipating God's glorious plan.

We have learned that though this is not the best of all possible worlds, God's marvelous plan is the only way to the best of all worlds. We have seen that God fulfills, beyond our wildest dreams, everything He promises.

"As I live," declares the Lord, "the whole world will be filled with the glory of the Lord."

Welcome home.

Welcome . . . to The Return of Heaven.

Afterward

Maybe This Isn't the End at All

Maybe this really isn't an afterword. Maybe it's the beginning—the beginning of asking questions that truly matter and refusing to settle for the small answers. Maybe it's like the stereogram. You have caught a glimpse of the truth—the real truth— for the first time and you have to start that journey up the spiral staircase of testing every action and every belief through the lens of this new truth.

This book was, in many ways, a labor of love. I didn't write it for an audience first—I wrote it for my grandchildren. For the ones who will come after me. For the ones who inherit a world full of noise but still carry that quiet ache for heaven. I wanted to leave something behind—something more than advice or opinions. I wanted to leave a story... one big enough to live inside, one sturdy enough to stand on, one clear enough to see through. And, at the end of the day, the only story that really matters. (For what does it profit a man to gain the whole world, yet lose his own soul?)

To my grandkids: I love each and every one of you with all my heart. This is for you. This is not just my story—it is our story. It is your story. This is who you are. Everything you will ever know, ever say, ever believe will flow through the truth in this story. Store it up in your heart. In the greatest days of your life, and in the deepest and darkest valleys of despair, hold on to this truth. Let it be your compass to guide you and your shield to protect you.

To my fellow seekers—we humans tend to compartmentalize everything. We sort our beliefs into bins and our questions into boxes, and sometimes—without meaning to—we miss the larger picture. We miss the deeper truth that connects it all. God is not a category. He is ultimate Reality—The Truth. And it changes how we see everything else. I hope this book helps you see that larger picture.

So, if you've made it this far, consider this a quiet invitation to keep seeking. Don't rush past the questions. Climb the spiral staircase—one step at a time—and see what comes into view. God invites you further in. There is more truth woven into your story than you can imagine. Everything you have experienced—everything that has shaped you into who you are—is a step in your journey to become the image-bearer He has always intended you to be. And if you seek Him with all your heart, you will find Him.

Throughout these pages, we've only been able to touch the surface of some very deep waters. Many of the questions raised here deserve more space than a single chapter—or even a single book—can hold. For that reason, I've created a companion space for anyone who feels drawn to continue the conversation.

There, you'll find a section called Keep Seeking—a growing collection of reflections, resources, and chapter-by-chapter explorations designed to walk with you as your questions unfold. It's not a place for quick answers or tidy conclusions. It's simply a place to wonder, to learn, to wrestle, and to grow—at your own pace.

You'll also find a way to reach out if something in this story stirred a question in you that won't easily rest. I may not have every answer, but I do read and listen, and I'll continue shaping future resources around the real questions people are carrying.

If and when you're ready, you can find it here:
www.TheReturnofHeaven.com

No pressure. No timeline. Just an open door.

Thank you for walking this far into the story with me. And wherever your next steps lead, may you continue to discover that the longing in you was never accidental.

Whether this becomes a series of books or simply a conversation that keeps growing, my prayer is this: that we would grow in wise love—learning how to love well, love deeply, and see one another through the eyes of the King who first loved us.

Jesus said,
"I am the way, and the truth, and the life. No one comes to the Father except through me."
(John 14:6, ESV)

Those words remain. And they still invite. They don't lead to rules and religion. They lead to transformation and eternal life.

Welcome to the journey.
Keep seeking, my friend.

NOTES

Chapter 1

1. No citations

Chapter 2

1. Jeremiah 29:13 (NASB)

2. Hebrews 11:1,6 (The Message)

Chapter 3

1. Francis Schaeffer, "The God Who Is There" (1968).

Chapter 4

1. 1 Corinthians 13:12 (NASB)

2. 1 Corinthians 15:37 (The Message)

Chapter 5

1. Job 1:6–12 (ESV)

2. Zechariah 3:1–2 (ESV)

3. Revelation 12:10 (ESV)

4. Genesis 3:1 (NASB)

5. Genesis 2:17 (ESV)

6. Genesis 3:6 (ESV)

7. Genesis 6:11–12 (ESV)

8. Deuteronomy 32:8–9

9. Ephesians 6:12

10. John 12:31 (NASB)

11. 1 John 2:16 (ESV)

Chapter 6

1. Ephesians 2:1

2. Genesis 11:4 (ESV)

3. Deuteronomy 32:8–9 (ESV)

4. Psalm 82:6–7 (ESV)

Chapter 7

1. Genesis 3:15

2. 2 Samuel 7:1–17

3. Isaiah 11:6–9

4. Daniel 7:13–14

5. Numbers 14:21

Chapter 8

1. See: Barry J. Beitzel, The New Moody Atlas of the Bible (2015), and Kenneth A. Kitchen, On the Reliability of the Old Testament (2003).

2. Deuteronomy 32:8–9 (ESV) and the division of the nations under spiritual rulers.

3. Deportation practices: Bright, J., "A History of Israel" (Westminster John Knox, 2000), pp. 340–343.

4. Jewish diaspora: Josephus, "Antiquities of the Jews" 11.5.

5. Psalm 137:1 & 4 (NASB)

6. Fall of Babylon to Cyrus: Herodotus, "Histories" 1.191; Xenophon, *Cyropaedia* 7.5.

7. Ezra 1:2 (NASB)

8. Cyrus Cylinder, British Museum (539 BC).

9. Spread of Koine Greek: Hengel, M., "Judaism and Hellenism" (Fortress Press, 1974).

10. Septuagint translation: "Letter of Aristeas" (2nd century BC).

11. Stoic philosophy on Logos: Marcus Aurelius, "Meditations"; Epictetus, "Discourses".

12. Philo of Alexandria, "On the Creation"; 'Who is the Heir of Divine Things?"

13. Antiochus IV Epiphanes' persecution: 1 Maccabees 1–2; 2 Maccabees 6–7.

14. Accounts of Jewish martyrdom: 2 Maccabees 7.

15. Hanukkah/rededication of the temple: 1 Maccabees 4:36–59; John 10:22.

16. Daniel 7:13–14 (NASB)

17. John 1:1,14 (NASB)

Chapter 9

1. Mathis, David. "God Grew Up in a Forgotten Town." Desiring God, December 6, 2018. https://www.desiringgod.org/articles/god-grew-up-in-a-forgotten-town

2. John 19:30 (ESV)

3. Luke 24:5–6 (ESV)

4. C.S. Lewis, "The Lion, the Witch, and the Wardrobe"— Allegory.

5. 2 Corinthians 1:20 (ESV)

Chapter 10

1. Colossians 1:13 (NASB).

2. See Colossians 1:13; Ephesians 5:8–9; 1 John 1:7 (NASB).

3. "Desperado", written by Glenn Frey and Don Henley.

4. Romans 7:15 (NASB).

5. Jeremiah 30:22 (NASB).

6. Matthew 28:18 (NASB).

7. Acts 1:8 (NASB).

8. Matthew 22:37–39 (NASB).

Chapter 11

1. Romans 6:23 (NASB)

2. Romans 1:24 (NASB)

3. 1 Thessalonians 4:13–18 (The Message)

4. John 8:36 (ESV)

5. 1 Corinthians 2:9 (NASB)

6. 2 Thessalonians 2:6–7 (NASB)

7. Matthew 24:8 (NASB)

8. Revelation 19:11–21 (NASB)

9. Genesis 1:3 (NASB)

10. Isaiah 11:6 (NASB)

11. Genesis 12:1–3 (NASB)

12. 2 Samuel 7:12–16 (NASB)

13. Amos 9:14–15; Isaiah 11:9 (NASB)

14. Revelation 20:11–15 (NASB)

Chapter 12

1. Psalm 82:7 (NASB).

2. 1 Corinthians 6:2–3 (NIV).

3. Revelation 20:11 (NASB).

4. Revelation 20:12a (NASB).

5. Revelation 20:12–13 (NASB).

6. Colossians 1:17 (NASB).

Chapter 13

1. Dr. Al McCallister, PhD, classroom lecture, Columbia International University, c. 1988–89.

2. John 17:24 (NASB)

3. John 14:1–3 (NASB)

4. Revelation 21:9–10 (NASB)

5. Revelation 21:24 (NASB)

6. Revelation 21:1 (NASB)

7. Revelation 21:24,26 (NASB)

8. 1 Corinthians 13:12 (NASB)

9. 1 John 3:2 (NASB)

10. Philippians 1:9–11 (NASB)

www.ingramcontent.com/pod-product-compliance
Lightning Source LLC
Chambersburg PA
CBHW030555130626
46552CB00006B/2554